THE CIVIL WAR

VOLUME 2

Camp life - Custer, George A.

GROLIER

Published 2004 by Grolier, an imprint of Scholastic Library Publishing
Sherman Turnpike
Danbury, Connecticut 06816

Set ISBN: 0-7172-5883-1
Volume ISBN: 0-7172-5885-8

Library of Congress Cataloging-in-Publication Data
The Civil War
        p.cm.
    Includes bibliographical references (p.) and index.
    Contents: v. 1. Abolition–Camp followers—v. 2. Camp life–Custer,
George A.—v. 3. Daily Life–Flags—v. 4.Florida–Hill, Ambrose P.—v. 5.
Home front, Confederate–Legacy of the Civil War—v. 6. Lincoln,
Abraham–Mobile Bay, Battle of—v. 7. Money and Banking–Politics,
Confederate—v. 8. Politics, Union–Shenandoah Valley—v. 9. Sheridan,
Philip H.–Trade—v. 10. Training–Zouaves.

    ISBN 0-7172-5883-1 (set: alk paper)—ISBN 0-7172-5884-X (v.1: alk paper)—
ISBN 0-7172-5885-8 (v.2: alk paper)—ISBN 0-7172-5886-6 (v.3: alk paper)—
ISBN 0-7172-5887-4 (v.4: alk paper)—ISBN 0-7172-5888-2 (v.5: alk paper)—
ISBN 0-7172-5889-0 (v.6: alk paper)—ISBN 0-7172-5890-4 (v.7: alk paper)—
ISBN 0-7172-5891-2 (v.8: alk paper)—ISBN 0-7172-5892-0 (v.9: alk paper)—
ISBN 0-7172-5893-9 (v.10: alk paper)

    1. United States—History—Civil War, 1861–1865—Encyclopedias,
Juvenile. [United States—History—Civil War, 1861–1865—
Encyclopedias.] 1. Grolier (Firm)

E468.C613 2004
973.7′03—dc22

2003049315

For information address the publisher:
Grolier
Sherman Turnpike,
Danbury, Connecticut 06816

FOR THE BROWN REFERENCE GROUP PLC
Project Editor: Emily Hill
Deputy Editor: Jane Scarsbrook
Designer: Paul Griffin
Picture Researcher: Becky Cox

Maps: David Atkinson
Indexer: Kay Ollerenshaw
Managing Editor: Tim Cooke
Consultants: Professor James I. Robertson Jr,
                               Virginia Technical Institute and
                               State University
                            Dr. Harriet E. Amos Doss,
                               University of Alabama in Birmingham

Printed and bound in Singapore

Text: Harriet Amos Doss, Charles Bowery, Cynthia
           Brandimarte, Tom Brown, Jacqueline Campbell,
           Gregg Cantrell, Chris Capozzola, Janet Coryell, Anita
           Dalal, Alan C. Downs, Larry Gara, Mark Grimsley,
           Anthony Hall, Tim Harris, Herman Hattaway, Edward
           Horton, R. Douglas Hurt, Ted Karamanski, Phil
           Katcher, Rachel Martin, Robert Myers, Henry
           Russell, John David Smith, Karen Utz, Chris Wiegand

ABOUT THIS BOOK

The Civil War was one of the turning points in U.S. history. The bitter "War between Brothers" cast a shadow that reaches to the present day. For the North the war began in determination to preserve the Union and ended as a crusade to free the slaves. For the South the conflict was the inevitable result of tensions between state and federal power that some argue remain unresolved. In its cavalry charges and sieges the war echoed wars of previous centuries; in its rifled weapons and its huge casualty figures—an estimated 620,000 soldiers died in four years of fighting—it looked forward to the world wars of the 20th century. This set of 10 books tells the stories of the key events, individuals, and battles of the struggle that split the nation. The alphabetically arranged entries also cover the social and political context of the fighting, and describe the involvement of every state in the war.

The Civil War was the first widely photographed war, and most of the images in the set were taken during the conflict itself. Most of the illustrations are also from contemporary sources, including the "special artists" who were sent to depict the battle action by newspaper editors. There are also numerous boxes giving eyewitness descriptions of individuals' experiences in battle or on the home front. Each entry ends with a list of cross-references to entries on related subjects elsewhere in the set. They will enable you to follow the subjects you are interested in and build your knowledge. At the end of each book there is a useful further reading list that includes websites, a glossary of special terms, and an index covering all 10 volumes.

Contents

Camp life

For all the weeks of the year spent on the march and fighting, there were months when the soldiers on both sides were living in camp and attending, in the words of one participant, "to the thousand commonplace duties of a soldier."

Above: Union soldiers outside a wedge tent. The wedge slept four men comfortably, but it was heavy. The lighter, two-man pup tent was used on campaign.

Right: A Civil War soldier's mess kit included a drum canteen for water, a tin plate, and a tin cup called a dipper.

To many new volunteers camp life and military discipline came as unpleasant surprises. When the war broke out, recruits from towns and cities throughout the country went to war expecting it to be an adventure. Many imagined they would join a local militia company with their friends and neighbors, spend a week or two learning basic drill, march off to meet the enemy, and perhaps be home within weeks. They did not sign up to spend time learning to be soldiers. Sergeant Vairin of the 2nd Mississippi Volunteers wrote in his diary on May 1, 1861, "Made my first detail … for guard duty to which most men objected because they said they did not enlist to do guard duty but to fight Yankees—all fun and frolic."

Fatigues and drill

The "fun and frolic" soon went out of soldiering when the hard work started. Bugles called reveille (wake-up) at 5:00 A.M. From then on for up to 16 hours a day it was an unceasing round of manual work, called fatigues, and repetitive weapon and marching exercises, called drill, until "lights out" at 9:00 P.M. Many found the rigid structure of their new lives difficult. One Confederate soldier wrote in his journal in 1862: "None can imagine, who has never experienced a soldier's life, the languor of mind, tediousness of time, as we resume day after day the monotonous duties."

Songs in camp

The men needed relief from army life, and camps were alive with diversions. Music was popular, either played by regimental bands or by the men themselves. Fiddles were highly prized, and music from banjos, flutes, and guitars was also common. The latest songbooks were found in the camps. The most popular songs tended to be either stirring tunes like the Union favorite "The Battle Cry of Freedom," for which the Southerners had their own version, or ballads like "Just before the Battle Mother," which tugged the heartstrings of that sentimental age.

Letters home

Writing letters was one of the most popular uses of soldiers' free time. Many men had never been away from their families before, and keeping in contact with home was vitally important. Literacy rates were high, particularly in Union regiments. For those who could not read or write a friend could always take dictation and read for them. Some regiments are said to have posted and received up to 600 letters in one day.

Camp sports

Soldiers played games that had originally come from England such as soccer and cricket, and organized races, wrestling, and boxing matches. The cavalry naturally held horse races whenever they could. In the winter the snow provided an outlet for pent-up energy, and snowball fights often broke out. They were large-scale exchanges in which whole regiments and even brigades took part. The biggest game in camp was baseball, either played on the diamond around four bases or around

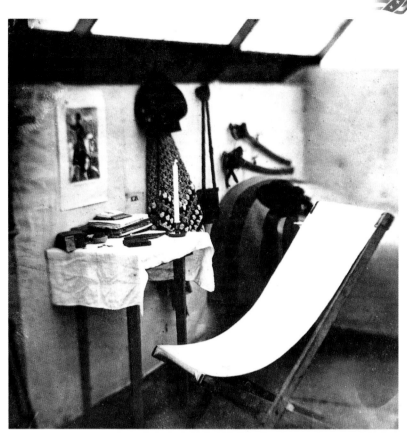

two bases, which was called townball. Officers and enlisted men played side by side, and in this way baseball lost its reputation as a gentlemen's game.

Gambling

If there was a competitive activity going on, someone, somewhere gambled on the winner. Gambling was strictly forbidden, but it was too widespread for officers to stop. Men bet on louse races, hog races, and even on toy boat races, but the favorites were dice and card games such as poker. On payday it was not unknown for a soldier to lose months of back pay on the walk from the pay tent to his quarters.

Sleeping under canvas

During the summer months the soldiers lived in tents. At the beginning of the war the Union army issued the wall tent. It was a very stable canvas tent

A cavalry officer's tent decorated with sabers on the wall and a crocheted shawl from home. Officers were allowed one trunk of personal belongings, which was carried in a baggage wagon.

held down by up to a dozen guy ropes, but it was complicated and took too long a time to pitch.

Another common type of tent, the wedge, was a triangular tent that could house four men comfortably. One of the most widely used was the Sibley, a high cone-shaped tent that could sleep a dozen men. It was too large and heavy to be taken on the march, however. On campaign the Union army used the two-man pup tent. Two men carried equal halves, which they buttoned together and pegged down at the end of a day on the move.

The Confederates were short of all resources, including tents. Most Southern soldiers on campaign improvised brushwood shelters called shebangs, often topped with half a pup tent captured from a Union soldier. Sometimes Confederate soldiers simply wrapped themselves in a blanket to get what sleep they could.

Winter camps

In the winter active campaigning became impossible because of the snow and mud, and encampments became semipermanent. Between December and March the armies settled down and built wooden huts, often complete with chimneys and doors. The army in camp became a small town with an array of camp followers to service the soldiers'

VISIT TO A CAMP

Confederate nurse Kate Cumming made the following journal entry on July 21, 1863, after visiting the 24th Alabama Regiment in camp:

"The regiment was encamped in a grove of trees; it had a few tents for the officers and commissary stores. But the only protection the men have from the inclement weather is their blankets put up on sticks about three feet high. The men were busy preparing for supper, and I did not think looked altogether pleased at my visiting them, as their attire and employment is not such as they would wish them to be. ... I could not help contrasting this camp with the one I last visited. It was when the war first commenced, and our house had been emptied of furniture to put in tents, as we thought it impossible for men to do without certain things which they had been accustomed to at home. Since then they have learned a few lessons, in this respect, as we all have."

needs. They ranged from the families of the officers to laundresses and sutlers (merchants) selling luxuries such as newspapers and tobacco.

A Union infantry camp in the war's eastern theater. The soldiers have built wooden huts to last the winter using trees from the surrounding woodland.

Carolina, North

North Carolina was the last state to secede from the Union. It suffered some of the gravest losses in the Civil War—both human and material—and the damage was not repaired for many years after the end of the hostilities.

North Carolina experienced a period of growth and prosperity between 1835 and 1860. The state helped finance the construction of roads and railroads, provided support for free public schools, and reformed the tax system. It also took steps toward granting legal status to women and liberalized criminal law. The outbreak of war brought these improvements to a sudden halt.

Secession

North Carolina stood by while the first seven states seceded from the Union in 1860 and early 1861, and took no part in the organization of the Confederacy at Montgomery, Alabama, in February 1861. Union sentiment was strong in the state, and many in North Carolina wanted to wait and see how events developed before committing themselves to one side or the other.

For a while it was unclear whether or not North Carolina would secede. However, its citizens reacted with hostility to the plan to use force to bring the seceded states back into the Union. As a result, when President Abraham Lincoln issued a general call for troops to fight the Confederacy after its bombardment and capture of Fort Sumter in April 1861, the majority of North Carolina's former Unionists and conservatives suddenly turned into secessionists and radicals.

When U.S. Secretary of War Simon Cameron requested two North Carolina regiments from Governor John W. Ellis, Ellis replied: "I regard the levy of troops

Union commander Ambrose E. Burnside in the port of New Bern, North Carolina, which he captured in early 1862. From mid-1862 the Union controlled most of the North Carolina coast.

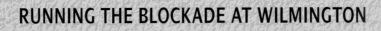
RUNNING THE BLOCKADE AT WILMINGTON

North Carolina led the Confederacy in blockade-running, and it was largely because of its success in defying the Union blockade at the port of Wilmington that Robert E. Lee was able to keep his army in the field as long as he did.

Wilmington was protected by Fort Fisher, a huge fort made largely of sand. Fort Fisher's massive guns kept the Union warships far enough out to sea to allow ships to run the blockade and supply the Confederacy.

The Union planned several attacks on Fort Fisher and Wilmington and finally attacked in December 1864. The attack, led by General Benjamin F. Butler, was repulsed. However, in January 1865 a combined land and sea assault was successful. The port was closed, cutting off the last Confederate supply line from the outside world.

Confederate forces defend Fort Fisher, the last major Southern stronghold. It fell to the Union on January 15, 1865.

by the administration for the purpose of subjugating the states of the South as in violation of the Constitution, and as a gross usurpation of power. I can be no party to this wicked violation of the laws of the country and to this war upon the liberties of a free people. You can get no troops from North Carolina."

On May 20, 1861, North Carolina became the last state to secede. When the secession was announced in the state capital, Raleigh, there was a hundred-gun salute, and everybody congratulated everybody else. North Carolina retained a streak of dissent, however. The state was one of the leading critics of the policies of the Jefferson Davis administration.

Eleven battles and 73 skirmishes were fought in the state, including several notable clashes. The Union victories at Fort Hatteras and New Bern in 1862 were part of a campaign that brought much of the coastal area under Union control by mid-1862. The fall of

Fort Fisher outside Wilmington in January 1865 was a great blow to the Confederacy (see box). The bloodiest battle in the state and one of the last major Confederate attacks of the war took place at Bentonville in March 1865, when Confederate General Joseph E. Johnston delayed Union General William T. Sherman's march north. On April 26, 1865, Johnston surrendered the last major Confederate army to Sherman near Durham.

Cost of the war

Although only a secondary theater of the war, North Carolina suffered some of the greatest losses of any state. The state contributed 125,000 men—more than one-sixth of all Confederate troops—in large part due to the efforts of Governor Zebulon B. Vance. Some 40,000 men from North Carolina were killed. The war also brought political division, social upheaval, and destroyed much of the state's wealth.

Carolina, South

South Carolina was the first state to secede from the Union, creating the spark that ignited the Civil War. It also saw the first outbreak of hostilities when Confederate forces bombarded Fort Sumter in Charleston Harbor in April 1861.

South Carolina had prospered in the 18th and 19th centuries as its slave-dependent agricultural base grew, especially its cotton plantations. Many planters switched from tobacco to cotton following the invention of the cotton gin in 1793. Using slave labor made cotton and rice growing very profitable. Although rice was not the state's major crop, half of the United States' rice was grown in Georgetown County alone. In 1860, on the eve of the Civil War, South Carolina was the third richest state in the country.

Declaration of secession

From the 1830s rumblings about secession from the United States grew as differences over trade, protective tariffs, and slavery increased between the industrializing states of the North and the largely agricultural, slave-owning South. Abraham Lincoln's election as president in November 1860 was the final straw for South Carolina's government. On December 20 that year state legislators signed the Ordinance of Secession in Charleston. On Christmas Eve Governor Wilkinson Pickens issued a proclamation declaring the state to be separate, independent, and sovereign. The declaration was an ultimatum to Union troops to leave.

During the following fortnight secessionists seized Fort Moultrie, Castle Pinckney, the arsenal at

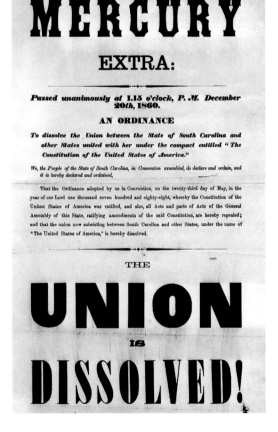

CHARLESTON

MERCURY

EXTRA:

Passed unanimously at 1.15 o'clock, P. M. December 20th, 1860.

AN ORDINANCE

To dissolve the Union between the State of South Carolina and other States united with her under the compact entitled " The Constitution of the United States of America."

We, the People of the State of South Carolina, in Convention assembled, do declare and ordain, and it is hereby declared and ordained,

That the Ordinance adopted by us in Convention, on the twenty-third day of May, in the year of our Lord one thousand seven hundred and eighty-eight, whereby the Constitution of the United States of America was ratified, and also, all Acts and parts of Acts of the General Assembly of this State, ratifying amendments of the said Constitution, are hereby repealed; and that the union now subsisting between South Carolina and other States, under the name of " The United States of America," is hereby dissolved.

THE

UNION

IS

DISSOLVED!

The Charleston Mercury, *a radical secessionist newspaper, announces South Carolina's departure from the Union on December 20, 1860.*

Charleston, and Fort Jackson without a shot being fired. There was a dramatic escalation in April, however, when Confederate forces bombarded Fort Sumter, in Charleston Harbor, for 34 hours before Major Robert Anderson surrendered. This action was the first serious engagement of the Civil War.

South Carolina was a hotbed of rebellion and a bastion of support for the Confederate cause. Although no

Union General William T. Sherman's troops burn McPhersonville on their march through South Carolina in February 1865.

major battles were fought on the state's soil, South Carolina provided many thousands of troops for the Confederate armies. It also suffered terrible casualties: York County lost 805 men out of a white male population of 4,379—around 20 percent—and such figures were mirrored across the state.

Union campaigns

There were two major Union campaigns to win back South Carolina. The first attempt started in July 1863 and dragged on for five months. The Union infantry landed by boats on the islands off the coast. Around 10,000 troops under the command of Quincy A. Gillmore, including the black soldiers of the 54th Massachusetts Infantry, attacked the forts around Charleston Harbor. Heavy bombardment from ironclads damaged the forts, and the 54th reached the inside of Fort Wagner in a courageous assault on July 18. But ultimately the attack was unsuccessful, and the regiment suffered withering losses. From October to mid-December Union guns blasted Fort Sumter almost daily—when Confederate President Jefferson Davis visited Charleston on November 2, he witnessed nearly 800

shells exploding around the beleaguered fortress. However, Fort Sumter's garrison still refused to surrender.

The second major campaign in South Carolina started in January 1865 after Union General William T. Sherman's March to the Sea, during which his army had stormed from Atlanta to Savannah in just five weeks, destroying everything in its path. Sherman vowed to push on through the Carolinas into Virginia. On January 19 he ordered a northward march into South Carolina. The state was considered to be the "cradle of secession," and many Union troops wanted to make it pay for being the cause of so much suffering.

Sherman in South Carolina

The 60,000 Union troops were opposed by the Confederate Army of Tennessee, led by Joseph E. Johnston and now numbering fewer than 10,000. Small units of Confederate infantry and cavalry harassed Sherman's forces, who also had to contend with felled trees, wrecked bridges, and the swollen Savannah River. Sherman misled the Confederates into thinking that he was marching to Charleston. Instead, he moved on to Columbia, which surrendered on February 17. As Union troops entered the city and Confederate troops left, fires were lit and much of the city burned. The identity of the culprits remains a matter of controversy.

Charleston was evacuated the same day, and a week later the railroad town of Camden fell to Union troops. By March they had reached the border with North Carolina. The Confederacy had effectively lost South Carolina. On April 14 the U.S. flag was raised once more over Fort Sumter—four years to the day after its surrender in 1861.

See also

Carpetbaggers and scalawags

Northerners who came South to the defeated Confederate states after the Civil War in search of political or personal gain were dubbed "carpetbaggers" and their Southern collaborators were known as "scalawags."

By 1870 all the former Confederate states had rejoined the Union, and in most the Republican Party ran the new state governments. The party only had support in the North before the Civil War, but it came to power in the postwar South largely because African American men gained the vote. They voted overwhelmingly for the Republican Party, and they were joined by groups of white men known as carpetbaggers and scalawags. With the backing of federal troops these groups controlled most Southern state governments during the period of Reconstruction (1865–1877).

Discrediting the Republicans

The terms "carpetbagger" and "scalawag" were coined by Democrats to discredit Southern Republicans. A carpetbagger was an uneducated, unprincipled Northern adventurer who came to the South to take advantage of the new political conditions in the defeated Confederacy. The name came from a common type of bag, called a carpetbag, which suggested that carpetbaggers were poor men who could carry all their belongings in this one bag. "They are fellows who crawled down South on the track of our armies … stealing and plundering," said Northern Democrat Horace Greeley.

The term "scalawag," meaning "scoundrel," was used for native Southerners who became Republicans after the war. Most white Southerners considered them to be traitors for supporting the party that had led the fight against the Confederacy and had imposed military rule on the defeated South after the war. In addition, scalawags were despised for collaborating with the other groups

A cartoon showing the South chained to occupying federal troops and being crushed by the policies of the Republican President Ulysses S. Grant, who is depicted riding in a huge carpetbag.

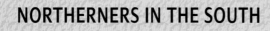
NORTHERNERS IN THE SOUTH

One high-profile carpetbagger was the Union General Adelbert Ames (*below*), who was appointed provisional governor of Mississippi after the war. The former Confederate state was one of the last to comply with the conditions of Reconstruction and rejoin the Union. Ames just managed to keep order during this time of near-anarchy, and he was elected governor when Mississippi was readmitted to the Union in 1870. However, he was accused of corruption by Democrats, and ill-feeling ran so high between Democrats and Republicans that riots broke out in Vicksburg on December 7, 1873.

Another beleaguered carpetbagger was Albion W. Tourgée, a former Union soldier who moved to North Carolina after the war. He was a lawyer and later a judge, and a steadfast supporter of freedmen's rights. By 1874 he had become a target of the Ku Klux Klan, but he continued to speak passionately about the sacrifice many blacks had made in the war and of "the Promised Land of your freedom!" to come. In 1879 Tourgée published a novel, *A Fool's Errand*, which describes the life of a Northerner in the South.

Adelbert Ames, the "carpetbagger" governor of postwar Mississippi.

making up the Southern Republican party, the Northern carpetbaggers and former slaves and free blacks.

Southern reaction

White Southerners were largely hostile to the new Republican governments, which they saw as artificial creations imposed on them from outside. They resented the tax increases placed on an already impoverished people and the widespread corruption among officials at all levels, especially in connection with railroad-building programs. They also resented the carpetbaggers' and scalawags' work to improve the social and political situation of freed slaves.

There are two contrasting views of carpetbaggers and scalawags. The traditional view supports the idea that they were corrupt opportunists motivated by greed, who manipulated blacks' new political power for their own ends. Historians point to the unrestrained corruption that characterized the South after the Civil War during the rule of the Southern Republican governments.

Other historians have challenged this assessment, however, suggesting that the carpetbaggers came to the South for a variety of reasons, and that many were not poor and desperate, but were teachers, lawyers, and businessmen. Some hoped to make money by farming or opening stores and businesses. Often they came with a sincere desire to help the former slaves. Some were agents of the Freedmen's Bureau, established to help former slaves make the transition to freedom.

Of the 60 carpetbagger politicians who served in Congress, 52 had served in the Union army. Many soldiers who had come to know the South during the war headed there in the postwar period to make a living. Some who had fought against slavery in the war wanted to make sure that the sacrifices were not in vain. When African American men gained the vote in 1867, it was not surprising that Northerners would become leaders in establishing the Republican Party in their new states.

Party politics

White Southern scalawags were likewise drawn to the Republican Party for a variety of reasons. Some were purely in search of opportunities to make money. But others had belonged to the Whig Party before the war and refused to join their political enemies, the Democrats, after the war. Some had opposed secession and remained pro-Union during the conflict. A few had even fought for the Union.

Many scalawags came from the poorer, more mountainous parts of their states. They believed that the prewar Democratic state governments had favored the wealthier plantation regions over their areas. A few wealthy planters were scalawags, especially in Mississippi and Louisiana, where they had been leaders of the prewar Whig Party. These scalawags were attracted to the Republicans' plans for building railroads and aiding the economic reconstruction of the South.

Republicans in power

After 1867, with former Confederate military and political leaders barred temporarily from voting or holding office, Republicans won election to hundreds of offices. Carpetbaggers served as governors of Arkansas, Louisiana, Mississippi, South Carolina, Georgia, and Florida, and 60 of them

were elected to Congress. Their election was often controversial. When carpetbagger William Kellogg became governor of Louisiana in 1872, many believed President Grant had fixed the election. On September 4, 1874, armed Democrats marched on the State House to overthrow the Kellogg government. Kellogg fled, and Grant sent 22 warships to restore peace. Adelbert Ames, a carpetbagger governor of Mississippi, also attracted hostility for corruption (see box).

Mixed record

As elected officials, carpetbaggers and scalawags had a mixed record. Some of them were involved in the corrupt schemes that brought the Southern Republican governments into disrepute. However, corruption was prevalent in the North and West during the Reconstruction era, as well as in the South. To their credit, the postwar Republican state governments did introduce several important reforms, such as a public school system and reform of taxes and the judiciary.

A Southern cartoon entitled "The murder of Louisiana" shows the 1872 election of carpetbagger William P. Kellogg as state governor. The Republican President Ulysses S. Grant watches over the proceedings—he was widely believed to have fixed the election.

See also

- Black Codes
- Freedmen
- Freedmen's Bureau
- Grant, Ulysses S.
- Ku Klux Klan
- Legacy of the Civil War
- Reconstruction
- Republican Party

Causes of the conflict

"On the subject of slavery the North and South are not only two Peoples, but they are rival, hostile Peoples," declared the *Charleston Mercury* in 1858. Slavery lay at the political, economic, and moral heart of the conflict.

A slave dealer's premises in Virginia, 1860. Slavery had existed in all 13 of the American colonies, but by the mid-19th century it was a purely Southern institution.

At the outbreak of war there was profound disagreement about what had brought the nation to the edge of conflict. Northern Unionists considered secession and the formation of the Confederate States to be an act of treason. They believed President Abraham Lincoln had no choice but to exert force to defend the Union. Southern secessionists, on the other hand, were outraged by the 1860 election of Lincoln, who had no support whatever in the South. As they saw it, the election made a mockery of the "United" in the nation's name. If the Southern states did not break away, their freedoms and their way of life would be trampled by a hostile North. If they could not go their separate way in peace, they were determined to defend themselves. To those on both sides, therefore, the war was justified as self-defense—defense of the Union on the one hand, defense of Southern freedoms on the other.

Slavery

This calamitous breakdown in relations between the Northern and Southern regions of the United States had been a long time coming—perhaps even since colonial times. The issue that was at the heart of the quarrel between them was the institution of black slavery.

Slavery existed in the American colonies from their earliest days in the 17th century. Slave labor was a central feature of the plantation system of agriculture. Colonists cultivated huge tracts of land to grow tobacco, sugar, rice, and later cotton. Such crops thrive in the warm climate and rich soil of the South. Cultivating these crops is labor intensive, however. The African slave trade allowed white settlers to buy the labor they needed. When the 13

SLAVERY AND THE CONSTITUTION

There was little discussion of the future of slavery when the Founders drew up the United States Constitution in 1787. Although the institution ran against the principles of liberty and equality on which the new republic was founded, "the thing is hid away in the constitution," as Lincoln said in 1854. In the 1850s antislavery campaigners accepted that they could not look to the Constitution to back their cause. Instead, William H. Seward, a New York senator, declared, "There is a higher law than the Constitution."

In 1787 Americans had focused on what united the different regions of their new nation, not what divided them. Northerners understood how important slavery was to the Southern economy and agreed that slaves were legally the property of their owners. One oblique mention of the matter in the Constitution concerned keeping hold of this property. Article IV, Section 2, stipulated that any "person held to service or labor in one state" could be reclaimed by his or her owner if he or she escaped to another state. With this in place Southern slaveholders felt no strong need to defend or justify the institution, as they would later. Many Southern slaveholders, however, had uneasy consciences. George Washington and Thomas Jefferson, for example, freed their own slaves in their wills.

American colonies declared their independence from Britain on July 4, 1776, there were about 600,000 slaves in the newly formed United States.

Almost all of these slaves were in the South. In the Northwest Ordinance of 1787 the federal government outlawed slavery in the region northwest of the Ohio River. This was no hardship since farming conditions were unsuitable for the large-scale plantation system. Small slave populations existed well into the 19th century in New York, New Jersey, and Pennsylvania, but slavery was very much a Southern institution.

By the early 19th century cotton was in great demand on the world market. Southern planters invested more money in land and slaves until the plantations dominated the Southern economy.

Expansion

The spectacular expansion of the United States during the first half of the 19th century brought the issue of slavery to the forefront of politics.

A frontier family in Kansas poses outside its home in the mid-19th century. As the country extended west, the issue of whether new states should allow slavery led to bloodshed in Kansas.

15

This map shows which side each state took in the Civil War. Of the four slave states that remained in the Union, Missouri, Kentucky, and Maryland had deeply divided loyalties. Troops from these states fought on both sides.

First the United States bought the Lousiana Territory from Emperor Napoleon Bonaparte of France in 1803. The transaction, known as the Louisiana Purchase, doubled the new nation's size. Then victory in the Mexican War (1846–1848) added another huge swath of territory in the west and southwest to the United States. In each case American settlers quickly moved the frontier west.

As the new territories became organized and more populous, they petitioned for statehood. The question arose, would slavery be permitted in these new states? Southern planters were desperate to extend slavery into the new territories. Growing cotton wore out the soil, and ever more land was needed to keep output high.

The politics of slavery

In 1819 predominantly Southern settlers in Missouri applied for entry to the United States with a state constitution that permitted slavery. This caused alarm in the North because Missouri lay almost entirely to the north of the existing division between free and slave states. Northern concerns at this stage were not about the morality of slavery but about political power. If the West beyond the Mississippi was open to slavery, then the South would be able to increase its voting strength in Congress. Southerners believed that if the West was closed to slavery, their way of life would be condemned to permanent minority status. Ominously for the future, the dispute in Congress was heated—voices on both sides threatened to break up the Union if the outcome was not to their satisfaction.

In 1820 a compromise was reached—the Missouri Compromise. By its terms Missouri was admitted as a slave state, and Maine in the North was admitted as a free state. In the remainder of the Louisiana Purchase slavery was permanently excluded north of latitude 36° 30'.

The Missouri Compromise held for a generation, but in the early 1850s it came under fire. Most of the territory ceded to the United States by Mexico lay south of 36° 30' and was potentially slave. There was a chorus of protest from the North about the seemingly limitless appetite of the South for extending slavery across the continent.

The abolition movement

There was growing sentiment among Northerners that slavery was a moral evil that must be removed or at least not allowed to spread. Such feelings were crystalized with the publication in 1852 of a novel by Harriet Beecher Stowe, a New England clergyman's daughter. *Uncle Tom's Cabin* presented a devastating picture of the cruelty of slavery and became a bestseller. Northerners who had previously cared little about the issue found themselves revolted by the idea that humans could be bought and sold like cattle. Those who called for the immediate freeing of Southern slaves were called abolitionists. These men and women were never more than a small minority in the North, but they were a loud and articulate minority. Southerners believed that by attacking slavery, abolitionists were attacking the entire Southern way of life. They responded by branding Stowe and her fellow abolitionists vile extremists who were encouraging slaves to rise up and murder their masters.

Rising tension

Extremist language characterized political debate and public argument in the 1850s. The more Northerners denounced slavery, the more Southerners defended it. Increasingly they did so without any apology for the "peculiar institution." They claimed that slavery was a moral good—that it was the natural condition of the "inferior" black race and a blessing for slave as well as master.

Kansas–Nebraska Act

In 1854 Congress passed the Kansas–Nebraska Act, which allowed two new territories to be created from the Louisiana Purchase, with the settlers entitled to decide for themselves on the issue of slavery. Popular sovereignty, as this principle was called, was in flat contradiction to the Missouri Compromise, since the territory in question lay north of 36° 30'. The Kansas–Nebraska Act set in train a series of crises that took the nation to the brink of war and beyond.

Kansas became a battlefield as proslavery men poured in from

A political poster for the Free Soil Party, led by Martin van Buren (far left). The party was set up in 1848 to oppose the adoption of slavery in territories won by the United States from Mexico. It later broke up, and most members joined the Republican Party, formed in 1854.

Abraham Lincoln's inauguration as president in Washington, D.C., in March 1861. The unfinished Capitol dome can be seen in the background.

See also

neighboring Missouri only to be confronted by Free Soilers (as antislavery settlers came to be called) from the East and the Midwest. The result was "Bleeding Kansas." Atrocities were committed by both sides, and both sides petitioned for statehood with constitutions that supported their views on slavery. The violence and political wrangling over Kansas continued up to the onset of the Civil War.

Dred Scott case

As the 1850s drew to a close, two incidents roused the pro- and antislavery forces to even greater heights of fury. In 1846 the Missouri slave Dred Scott had sued for his freedom on the grounds that he had in the past resided with his master in a free state and a free territory for several years. The case dragged on until it finally reached the Supreme Court in 1856. In its judgment, given the following year, the Court decreed that Scott was still a slave, that blacks were not United States citizens, and that laws banning slavery in parts of the

territories (specifically the Missouri Compromise) were unconstitutional. Antislavery forces were aghast. No Supreme Court ruling has created such uproar as the Dred Scott decision.

John Brown

Any Southern optimism that the slavery controversy would go away was shattered in October 1859. John Brown, an abolitionist crusader, led a raid on the federal arsenal at Harpers Ferry in Virginia. His aim was to lead a slave uprising that would sweep the South once he was able to provide local slaves with arms. The raid was a bloody fiasco, and after a two-day siege a badly wounded Brown was captured. He was convicted of murder and hanged a few weeks later. Despite John Brown's violent fanaticism—he and his sons had butchered several proslavery men in Kansas—the noble bearing Brown presented at his trial gained him sympathy in the North. To Southerners the elevation of a murderer to the status of a martyr in the North was proof that their fellow-countrymen despised them. Many believed it was time to go their separate way.

A new president

The election of Abraham Lincoln of the Republican Party as president in November 1860 dismayed the South. Lincoln and the Republicans, a new political party that drew all its support from the North and the West, had campaigned strongly against any extension of slavery. To accept such an electoral verdict was, to most Southerners, to accept second-class status in the Union. Secession seemed the only answer, and so the fateful step was taken.

Cavalry

In 1860 there were only five regiments of cavalry in the U.S. Army. By the end of the war the Union had more than 170 cavalry regiments, while the Confederates had more than 130 cavalry regiments and 100 **independent cavalry battalions.**

Like the infantry, the basic cavalry component on both sides was a regiment commanded by a colonel. A Confederate cavalry regiment was made up of some 10 companies of between 60 to 80 men. In the Union army a cavalry regiment had about 1,000 men divided into six squadrons, each containing two troops of up to 100 men. The organization was simplified in 1863, and the squadron was replaced by battalions of four troops each.

Every cavalry regiment had a blacksmith and a farrier (who shoed the horses). A Union cavalry regiment also took along a surgeon, his assistant, and two hospital stewards—luxuries most Confederate outfits could not afford. The numbers in each unit varied widely on campaign, since most cavalry units, particularly on the Confederate side, were always understrength.

Horses

One of the great differences between the Union and Confederate cavalry was that Southern troopers had to supply their own horses. The system worked well enough in the first years of war, because the South was largely rural, and most volunteers could supply their own mounts. As the war went on and losses of horses through battle, sickness, and sheer exhaustion took their toll, the numbers of Confederate cavalry dwindled as cavalrymen who had no horse to ride had to leave their companies to find new mounts.

Union cavalry accompany artillery units maneuvering a field-gun carriage during the advance on Petersburg, Virginia, in June 1864.

Attempts by the army to make these men fight on foot as infantry usually failed—most cavalrymen would sooner desert than become infantrymen.

The Union government also started the war asking volunteer regiments to supply their own horses as a way of saving money. Cavalry were the most expensive soldiers to equip—a single regiment might cost up to $600,000. By July 1863 a new supply system had been imposed in the Union army. The War Department established the Cavalry Bureau to buy mounts for the cavalry. Within a year 150,000 horses had been purchased and supplied through two depots, one in Washington, D.C., and one in St. Louis, Missouri.

Cavalry weapons

The three basic cavalry weapons used in the war were the saber, the carbine, and the pistol. A notable exception was the 10-foot wooden lance carried by the 6th Pennsylvania Cavalry, a regiment known as Rush's Lancers. The regiment had abandoned this out-of-date European weapon—unused—by 1863.

The saber, with its 3-foot-long (90-cm) curved blade, was designed to be the cavalryman's principal offensive weapon. But many Confederate cavalrymen, such as the Virginia raider John S. Mosby, regarded it in the same way as the lance. He wrote after the war "My men were as little impressed by a body of cavalry charging them with sabers as though they had been armed with cornstalks." Confederate cavalrymen preferred large-caliber pistols such as the six-shot Colt Navy, although Union cavalry continued to carry sabers throughout the conflict and found that they could still be effective in close combat.

The Union cavalry had the edge in firepower when it came to the carbine. There were various patterns of this short-barreled weapon. One of the most common types used by the Union cavalry was the Sharps. The most advanced carbine was the Spencer breechloading repeater, which could fire seven rounds before reloading. By 1865 the Union army had issued over 80,000 Sharps and 90,000 Spencers to

A recruitment poster for the New York Cavalry. At the start of the war the Union had far fewer skilled horsemen than the Confederacy. Some recruits had to learn to ride after they enlisted.

its cavalrymen. In contrast, the Confederates began the war with muzzleloaders and even shotguns. Most of the breechloaders they used later were captured from Union forces.

Cavalry tactics

The breechloading carbine was one of the reasons why cavalry tactics changed so much as the war went on. In 1861 it was still believed that a line of saber-wielding troopers could drive infantry off the battlefield in a single charge. The Confederate cavalry commander J.E.B. Stuart achieved this feat at the First Battle of Bull Run (Manassas) on July 21, 1861, when his 1st Virginia Cavalry routed the 11th New York Zouaves, though this had more to do with the Union infantrymen's inexperience in combat. Later in the war veteran infantry would stand firm behind cover and rely on the range and power of their rifle muskets to fend off a cavalry charge. In previous wars infantry stood little chance of surviving a charge of cavalry, but Civil War

infantry with rifled muskets accurate up to 300 yards (275m) could turn a cavalry attack into a suicide charge.

H. Kyd Douglas, a Confederate officer, described one such experience in the Shenandoah Valley in 1862: "Just as these hundred men had reached the fence, the cavalry came thundering by, but a deadly volley stopped their wild

Union officers of C and D companies, 1st Massachussetts Cavalry, near Petersburg, Virginia, August 1864.

A CAVALRYMAN'S BELONGINGS

In April 1861, as volunteers mustered for the first time, many carried more gear than they could cope with. A Confederate cavalryman recruited into the W.P. Rangers, a Texas cavalry company, remembered his baggage even before he received his official weapons and ammunition:

"Myself, saddle, bridle, saddle-blanket, curry comb, horse brush, coffee pot, tin cup, 20 lbs. of ham, 200 biscuits, 5 lbs. ground coffee, 5 lbs. sugar, one pound cake presented to me by Mrs. C. E. Talley, 6 shirts, 6 pairs socks, 3 pairs draws, 2 pairs pants, 2 jackets, 1 pair heavy mud boots, one Colt's revolver, one small dirk [dagger], four blankets, sixty feet of rope with a twelve inch iron pin attached … and divers and sundry little mementoes from friends."

A skirmish between Confederate and Union cavalry during a raid. The cavalry of both sides carried out raids behind enemy lines, raising morale by their daring exploits.

Cavalry raids

Denied their traditional role as shock-troops and battle-winners, by 1862 the cavalries of both armies were struggling to find a new contribution to make. The Union cavalry was still a very young and inexperienced force and was mainly used to guard supply lines and encampments. The Confederate cavalry, which had better leadership and finer horsemen, began to specialize in large-scale raids and reconnaissance operations, such as J.E.B. Stuart's ride around George B. McClellan's Union army (see box). As the war went on, cavalry units from both sides served behind the lines as guerrilla fighters.

Raids behind enemy lines, distracting and confusing the enemy, did wonders for the cavalry's reputation and raised morale. However, while the cavalry was raiding, it could not concentrate on its other vital but less glamorous task of keeping a watch on the enemy's movements. This failure had serious consequences in later battles. At Chancellorsville in May 1863 Union General Joseph Hooker sent his cavalry away on a raid and, as a result, was

career. Some in front, unhurt, galloped off, on their way, but just behind them horses and riders went down in a tangled heap. The rear, unable to check themselves, plunged on in, over upon the bleeding pile, a roaring, shrieking, struggling mass of men and horses, crushed, wounded and dying. It was a sickening sight, the worst I had ever seen then, and for a moment I felt a twinge of regret that I had ordered that little line to that bloody work."

STUART'S RIDE AROUND McCLELLAN

One of the most spectacular cavalry raids took place in June 1862, when J.E.B. Stuart, by then a brigadier general and Confederate General Robert E. Lee's cavalry chief, took 1,200 men on a daring three-day ride around Union General George B. McClellan's army encamped on the Virginia Peninsula outside Richmond.

Stuart awoke his cavalrymen at 2:00 A.M. on the first day of the ride and told them to be in the saddle in ten minutes. In all, the Confederates rode 100 miles (160km) around the 100,000-strong Union army, taking prisoners, plundering

supplies, and sabotaging railroad tracks. Stuart also brought back valuable information to Lee about the position of McClellan's army. During the entire raid he lost only one of his men and one piece of artillery.

The raid was hailed as a great success and an example of Southern dash and courage, giving the Confederates a boost in morale and further enhancing Stuart's reputation. One of Stuart's staff officers recalled, "Everywhere we were seen, we were greeted with enthusiasm. General Stuart's name was praised and celebrated in every manner."

not warned of the arrival of Lee's army from Fredericksburg. Two months later in Pennsylvania Lee himself was let down by J.E.B. Stuart, who, in an attempt to repeat his exploit on the peninsula was not in a position to warn his commander that the Union army was concentrating at Gettysburg.

These failures were partly responsible for the cavalry's poor reputation among the infantry of both sides, who were doing most of the fighting and dying. "Whoever saw a dead cavalryman?" was a common infantry jibe, while in 1864 one disgruntled Confederate soldier wrote: "I do wish the Yankees would capture all the cavalry ... they never will fight so I think it is useless to have them in the army eating rations."

New tactics
During 1863 the Confederate cavalry began to decline, as their numbers and fighting quality suffered through a lack of new recruits, horses, and weapons. The Union cavalry, on the other hand, were growing in number, confidence, and experience, and were taking a more offensive role by adopting the tactics of mounted infantry. Their horses gave the troopers mobility on the battlefield, while the carbine, especially the Spencer, gave them the firepower to hold positions against Confederate infantry when fighting on foot.

Union cavalry at Gettysburg
Two brigades of John Buford's 1st U.S. Cavalry Division, fighting in this way, held off two Confederate divisions on the first day of the Battle of Gettysburg on July 1, 1863. From cover behind a stone wall the cavalrymen fought for two hours until reinforced by infantry, making sure that the Army of the Potomac held the high ground that in the end proved decisive to the outcome of the battle.

This was not cavalry warfare in the classic saber-charging European style, but it suited the Civil War soldier and the kinds of battle he fought. In later decades it helped change cavalry tactics around the world.

Alfred Pleasonton (right) and George A. Custer, two of the Union's best cavalry commanders, in Falmouth, Virginia, April 1863.

See also

- Brandy Station, Battle of
- Buford, John
- Custer, George A.
- Forrest, Nathan B.
- Gettysburg, Battle of
- Grierson's Raid
- Guerrilla warfare
- Horses
- Mosby, John S.
- Pleasonton, Alfred
- Reconnaissance
- Stuart, J.E.B.

Cedar Mountain, Battle of

A detachment of the Confederate Army of Northern Virginia under Thomas J. "Stonewall" Jackson clashed with part of John Pope's new Union Army of Virginia led by Nathaniel P. Banks on August 9, 1862, in Culpeper County, Virginia.

When Robert E. Lee contemplated his course of action following the Seven Days' Campaign in June 1862, he looked to one of his chief subordinates, Thomas J. "Stonewall" Jackson, to help him solve a strategic problem. As Lee faced the Union Army of the Potomac near Richmond, another Union army was forming under John Pope near Washington, D.C. A unit of this new Army of Virginia was led by a political appointee, Nathaniel P. Banks.

In late July Pope sent Banks with 12,000 soldiers to threaten the Virginia Central Railroad, a vital Confederate supply line. Lee reacted by sending Jackson with three divisions, totaling 22,000 troops, to deal with Banks.

Union General Samuel J. Crawford's brigade advances at the Battle of Cedar Mountain. Greatly outnumbered, the brigade's determined attack almost prevailed against the Confederate forces.

Jackson and Banks were old rivals. A few months earlier the two generals had faced off in the Shenandoah Valley. Now Jackson relished the chance to strike at his Union enemies again. On August 9 he positioned his troops on the northwest of Cedar Mountain in anticipation of a battle.

The day of battle

Jackson had outmaneuvered and defeated Banks before, but this time the battle began differently. Jackson's secretiveness over his orders caused confusion, and the Confederate forces arrived on the battlefield in a piecemeal condition. Jackson himself added to the confusion by spending hours placing artillery pieces on the right side of his line. Charles S. Winder was left to deploy his division on the Confederate left flank in a stand of trees.

The artillery of both sides began the battle and carried out an inconclusive duel while the infantry forces deployed. Banks attacked the left of Jackson's infantry line as it was forming. Winder was killed almost immediately, and the troops under his command crumbled in the face of an energetic Union attack from a unit only a fraction of their size. For a time the Confederate position was critical, as the advancing Union forces under Samuel J. Crawford threatened to separate Winder's and Jubal A. Early's divisions from that of

Ambrose P. Hill, which was still arriving on the field. On the march to Cedar Mountain, Hill and Jackson had quarreled, but this disagreement was forgotten for the moment. The arrival of Hill's division turned the tide. His five brigades made it to the field and marched straight into battle.

The Confederates rally

In a stirring display of bravery Jackson rallied his retreating troops in person. At one point he tried to pull his sword from its scabbard, only to find that it had rusted in place. Removing his sword and its scabbard from his belt and waving it in the air, he then took a battle flag from a soldier and waved it, shouting, "Jackson is with you!" His example, combined with arriving reinforcements, changed temporary Union success into defeat. The attacking Union forces, tired and disorganized from marching and fighting on a hot day, gave way before the Confederate counterattack and left the field by nightfall. At a cost of 1,400 casualties Jackson's force had defeated Banks and his men, inflicting 2,500 Union casualties in the process.

Although Jackson later declared that Cedar Mountain was "the most successful of his engagements," it was actually Hill's counterattack that led to victory. Jackson's own faulty dispositions and failure to attend to his left flank had almost cost him defeat at the hands of an enemy whom he outnumbered by two to one.

Two days later Jackson fell back to his base at the railroad junction at Gordonsville, where he awaited the arrival of Lee and the rest of the Army of Northern Virginia. Lee, Jackson, and James Longstreet were reunited on August 15 and began planning a strike against the rest of Pope's Army of Virginia. This resulted in the campaign and battle of Second Bull Run at the end of August 1862.

A Union battery fords a tributary of the Rappahannock River on the day of battle, August 9, 1862.

See also

- Banks, Nathaniel P.
- Early, Jubal A.
- Hill, Ambrose P.
- Jackson, Thomas J.
- Lee, Robert E.
- Northern Virginia, Army of
- Pope, John
- Potomac, Army of the
- Bull Run (Manassas), Second Battle of
- Seven Days' Campaign
- Shenandoah Valley

Chamberlain, Joshua L.

Joshua Lawrence Chamberlain (1828–1914) was one of the Union's military heroes during the Civil War. He fought with courage in many major battles. He was wounded six times—once near fatally—and had six horses shot from under him.

Ulysses S. Grant chose Chamberlain to receive the formal surrender of weapons and colors from Lee's Army of Northern Virginia on April 12, 1865.

Joshua Lawrence Chamberlain was born at Brewer, Maine, on September 8, 1828, and educated at Bowdoin College and Bangor Theological Seminary. For years he taught rhetoric and oratory at Bowdoin, but in 1862, at age 34, he volunteered for military service and joined the 20th Maine Infantry as a lieutenant colonel. The 20th Maine served with the Army of the Potomac through most of its engagements in the Civil War.

A glorious career

At Fredericksburg Chamberlain and his men came under continuous Confederate fire for hours on the night of December 13, 1862. This was just the beginning of Chamberlain's outstanding war. At the Battle of Gettysburg (July 1–3, 1863) he led his regiment in defense of Little Round Top, a small wooded hill on the far left of the Union line. For holding this key position in the face of repeated enemy attacks, and for leading a bayonet charge when his men ran out of ammunition, Chamberlain was awarded the Congressional Medal of Honor in 1893.

During Union assaults on Petersburg in June 1864, Chamberlain so impressed Ulysses S. Grant with his bravery that Grant promoted him to brigadier general in the field. Although wounded during the battle, Chamberlain soon returned to the front. On April 12, 1865, he was breveted major general. On the same day he had the honor of receiving the formal surrender of Robert E. Lee's men. As the Confederate soldiers handed over their arms, Chamberlain chivalrously brought his own men to attention to salute their beaten foe.

After the Civil War Chamberlain refused a commission in the regular army. Instead, he served as governor of Maine (1866–1870) and was then president of Bowdoin College from 1871 to 1883. He spent his later years as a businessman and was involved in the construction of a railroad in Florida. He also wrote extensive reminiscences of the war, including *The Passing of the Armies* (1915). Chamberlain died in Portland, Maine, on February 24, 1914.

See also

- Fredericksburg, Battle of
- Gettysburg, Battle of
- Medals and honors
- Petersburg, Siege of
- Potomac, Army of the
- Surrender of the Confederacy

Chancellorsville, Battle of

The Battle of Chancellorsville saw Robert E. Lee's Confederate Army of Northern Virginia fight the Union Army of the Potomac led by Joseph Hooker on May 1–4, 1863. The battle is often regarded as the best example of Lee's tactical brilliance.

Through the winter of 1862–1863 the Union Army of the Potomac and the Confederate Army of Northern Virginia faced one another across the Rappahannock River at Fredericksburg, Virginia. The Union army had failed to take the city in a disastrous battle in December 1862. Union morale improved with the appointment of a new commander, Joseph Hooker, in January 1863.

Hooker's plan

Hooker reorganized the army and came up with a new plan of campaign for the spring. Instead of attempting a frontal attack on the Confederate positions overlooking Fredericksburg, Hooker divided his army and took half of it— three corps totaling 75,000 men—to cross the river at fords upstream and come around in a wide sweep to attack Lee's army from behind. John Sedgwick stayed at Fredericksburg with 40,000 men to hold the Confederates.

By April 30 the Union troops had crossed the river and were in a dense area of woodland called the Wilderness. The center of their position was a crossroads at Chancellorsville, Virginia. Hooker's plan had worked smoothly so far, but now things started to go wrong.

Lee realized that Hooker was trying a flanking march. On April 29 he sent two brigades toward Chancellorsville to discover the size of the threat. Once they confirmed the Union army was at Chancellorsville, he went on the attack. Like Hooker, Lee divided his forces, leaving 10,000 men under Jubal A. Early to hold Fredericksburg and marching his remaining 50,000 men west to meet Hooker.

Hooker was taken by surprise on May 1 when the Confederates started an attack on his lead divisions at noon. The Union commander began to lose his nerve. In midafternoon he halted the advance and ordered his forces back to Chancellorsville to take up defensive positions.

Jackson's flanking march

Lee now had the initiative. In one of the war's boldest moves he divided his army once again early on May 2. He

The shooting of Stonewall Jackson on May 2 during the battle of Chancellorsville. He was accidentally shot by his own men as he returned to his lines in the evening. His arm was amputated, but he died a few days later.

Battle details

1. In a brilliant maneuver the Union army marched north from Fredericksburg, crossed the river, and took up positions around the Chancellorsville crossroads by April 30.

2. On May 2 Jackson surprised and routed the Union right flank.

3. On May 3 fighting took place at both Chancellorsville and Fredericksburg, where Union forces attacked and drove the Confederates away and advanced to Salem Church.

4. Lee turned his army around to stop this advance and defeated the Union troops. On May 5 and 6 Union forces retreated across the river.

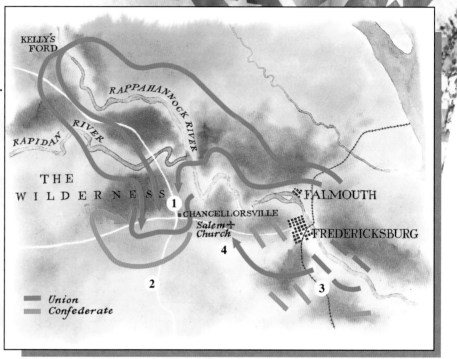

sent Thomas J. "Stonewall" Jackson and 28,000 men on a 12-mile (19-km) march to strike Hooker's right flank, while his remaining troops faced three Union corps.

Jackson's flanking march

The march took all day, but at 6:00 P.M. Jackson attacked the Union XI Corps, which broke and ran. Only nightfall saved Hooker's army. That evening Jackson was shot by his own men who mistook his party for Union cavalry.

J.E.B. Stuart temporarily took over Jackson's command and on May 3 reopened the attack while Lee struck from the south. The Union line was pushed back from Chancellorsville north toward the river. Hooker was stunned when a shell exploded near him and handed over command to Darius Couch.

The Union troops were facing total defeat. However, at Fredericksburg on May 3 the remaining Union troops under Sedgwick had attacked and driven away Early's troops. Sedgwick now advanced west to come to Hooker's aid. With Hooker in retreat on May 4 Lee turned to attack Sedgwick. At Salem Church the Confederates halted the Union advance.

Hooker withdrew across the river on the night of May 5. His defeat by an army half his size cost more than 17,000 casualties. Lee's losses were 12,800, including the irreplaceable Jackson, who died a few days later.

Charleston

Charleston was a Confederate stronghold, and was at the hub of events leading up to the Civil War. The opening engagement of the war took place in Charleston harbor on April 12–14, 1861, when Confederate forces captured Fort Sumter.

Charleston, South Carolina, was in the vanguard of the struggle for states' rights from the beginning of the dispute to the formation of the Confederacy. South Carolina became the first state to break away from the Union when the Ordinance of Secession was passed by a convention of elected citizens in Charleston on December 20, 1860.

Union attacks

Charleston was well protected by Fort Sumter and other lesser fortifications, and withstood several naval assaults during the early months of the war. Union Rear Admiral Samuel F. Du Pont launched a major assault on April 7, 1863. He attacked the city with a flotilla of seven monitor warships and two other ironclads. However, the ships were driven back by 77 Confederate cannons on Fort Sumter and ran into the harbor's mines and obstructions. Du Pont was forced to withdraw. He decided against renewing his attack the next day after one of the ironclads, the USS *Keokuk*, sank during the night.

Long siege

Union land and sea forces then laid siege to Charleston for 20 months. On July 10, 1863, Union troops under Quincy A. Gillmore landed on Morris Island in the south of the harbor, but Confederate resistance was so great that they did not capture the batteries there until September 7. Meanwhile, the Union bombarded Fort Sumter relentlessly but failed to capture it.

Charleston remained blockaded until 1865. The deadlock was broken when William T. Sherman cut off the city's communications with the interior as he marched north through the Carolinas. Confederate commander Pierre G.T. Beauregard ordered the garrison to evacuate, and the troops withdrew on the night of February 17. The citizens panicked, and chaos engulfed the city. Much damage was caused, as cotton was burned and military installations blew up. Union forces took control of the ravaged city the following morning.

A view from the Circular Church in Charleston after the evacuation of Confederate troops in February 1865.

See also

- Beauregard, Pierre G.T.
- Carolina, South
- Fortifications
- Secession
- Siege warfare
- States' rights
- Sumter, Fort
- Union navy

Chattanooga, Battle of

The city of Chattanooga, Tennessee, assumed great strategic importance for both sides during the Civil War. The fight to gain control of the city began in June 1863, culminating in the Battle of Chattanooga on November 23–25.

Chattanooga in southeastern Tennessee lay at the rail junction linking Virginia with Tennessee, Georgia, and points west. Without this vital rail terminus Confederate troops moving between different theaters of war would have to use a roundabout series of railroads in the Deep South. For the Union Chattanooga was an objective because it could serve as a base for an attempt to capture Atlanta. As the war went on, it became clear that whoever controlled Chattanooga was in a position to control Tennessee, Georgia, and Alabama.

The railroad at Chattanooga, with Lookout Mountain in the background. Chattanooga was a vital junction on the main east–west route in the Confederacy.

Union occupation
Between June and August 1863 Union General William S. Rosecrans and his Army of the Cumberland had opened up central and eastern Tennessee and driven Confederate General Braxton Bragg and his Army of Tennessee out of Chattanooga. The Confederates checked the Union advance at the Battle of Chickamauga (September 19–20), forcing the Army of the Cumberland back to Chattanooga. Bragg then laid siege to the city.

The outlook for the Union forces was grim, as their supplies quickly began to run out. The Confederates were unable to muster the strength to attack, however, and Lincoln reinforced the city with additional troops. In October Ulysses S. Grant arrived to resolve the situation. He reinvigorated his forces by restoring their supply lines and making efforts to dislodge the Confederates from the fortifications around the city.

Battle details

1. On October 26 Union forces established the "cracker" line to supply the Army of the Cumberland besieged in Chattanooga.
2. On November 23 Union troops dislodged the Confederates from their position on Orchard Knob, a foothill below Missionary Ridge.
3. Union troops then attacked Lookout Mountain in thick fog on November 24 and drove away Confederate forces.
4. Union forces converged on Missionary Ridge on November 25 and by 4:00 P.M. had routed Bragg's Confederates.

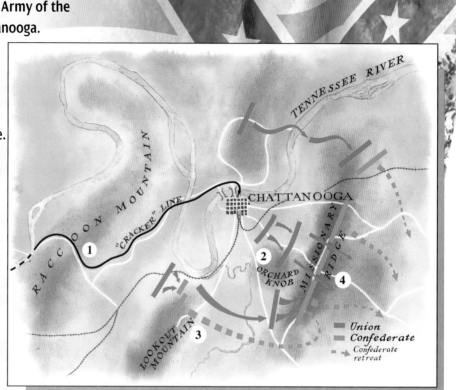

The Battle above the Clouds

On November 23 the Army of the Cumberland crossed the Tennessee River at several points in an attempt to break the Confederate siege. The offensive succeeded. Elements of Grant's army scaled Lookout Mountain and on November 24 fought what became known as the Battle above the Clouds, which forced Bragg out of a key position above Chattanooga.

Missionary Ridge

Following defeat at Lookout Mountain, Bragg entrenched on Missionary Ridge, a strong position stretching south from the Tennessee River. Bragg's generals placed their men in poor positions, however. In one of the war's most stunning victories Union troops under George H. Thomas stormed Missionary Ridge on November 25 and defeated the Confederates. With no safe positions left, Bragg retreated south along the rail line to Atlanta in order to protect that key supply artery.

Union victory

The battles for Chattanooga were over. In six months Union armies had taken control of the "Gateway to the South" and changed the course of the war. Union forces under William T. Sherman now had the supply base and jumping-off point they needed to initiate a campaign against Atlanta.

For the Confederacy the loss of Chattanooga completed their loss of the rail networks, food supplies, and manpower of central Tennessee.

See also

- Atlanta, Fall of
- Bragg, Braxton
- Chickamauga, Battle of
- Grant, Ulysses S.
- Kennesaw Mountain, Battle of
- Railroads
- Tennessee
- Thomas, George H.
- West, the Civil War in the

Chesnut, Mary B.

Mary Chesnut (1823–1886) wrote the most famous account of the Confederate home front. She organized and revised her journal entries into book form after the war, but the journal was not published until 1905, 19 years after her death.

Mary Boykin Miller was born on March 31, 1823, into a wealthy South Carolina planter family. She married a young lawyer, James Chesnut Jr., in 1840. In 1858 James Chesnut was elected to the U.S. Senate. The couple moved to Washington, D.C., where they were close to Jefferson and Varina Davis—later to become the first family of the Confederacy. When the Republican Abraham Lincoln was elected president in 1860, James Chesnut resigned. The couple returned to South Carolina, where James worked on the state's ordinance of secession.

Mary's journal

Early in 1861 Mary Chesnut began to keep a journal. Her husband's career placed her at excellent vantage points. She was in Charleston for the bombardment of Fort Sumter, where she wrote, "I do not pretend to go to sleep. How can I? If Anderson [the Union garrison commander] does not accept terms—at four—the orders are he shall be fired upon. … At half past four, the heavy booming of a cannon. I sprang out of bed. And on my knees … I prayed as I never prayed before."

The Chesnuts soon moved to the new Confederate capital of Richmond. Her journal is a spirited account of the city's upper classes during the war. She wrote about "starvation parties" where hostesses served only water and about fine ladies selling clothes to buy food when the Confederate currency became worthless. Chesnut also wrote movingly about the turning tide of the war. When Atlanta fell to the Union in September 1864, Chesnut despaired: "Since Atlanta I have felt as if all were dead within me, forever. … We are going to be wiped off the earth."

After the war the Chesnuts were heavily in debt, and their old home was a shell. In the 1870s Mary revised her diary to make a book, but it was not published until after her death.

See also

- Atlanta, Fall of
- Charleston
- Confederate government
- Davis, Jefferson
- Home front, Confederate
- Plantation life
- Secession

DISCUSSION WITH DAVIS

An extract from Chesnut's journal entry for April 17, 1861:

"In Mrs. Davis's drawing-room last night, the President took a seat by me on the sofa where I sat. He talked for nearly an hour. He laughed at our faith in our own powers. … We think every Southerner equal to three Yankees at least. We will have to be equivalent to a dozen now. … He believes that we will do all that can be done by pluck and muscle, endurance, and dogged courage. … And yet … there was a sad refrain running through it all. For one thing, either way, he thinks it will be a long war. That floored me at once. It has been too long for me already."

Chickamauga, Battle of

The Union Army of the Cumberland, commanded by William S. Rosecrans, fought Braxton Bragg's Confederate Army of Tennessee at Chickamauga on September 19–20, 1863. The battle was part of the campaign to gain control of Chattanooga.

Rosecrans's Union Army of the Cumberland forced Bragg's Confederates out of central Tennessee in the Tullahoma Campaign of June 1863. The Confederates fell back to Chattanooga, in southeastern Tennessee, a key rail junction on the main Confederate east-west railroad. After the Union victories at Gettysburg and Vicksburg the administration hoped the capture of Chattanooga would deal the finishing blow to the Confederacy. In an almost bloodless campaign Rosecrans's army crossed the Tennessee River at several points south of the city and managed to compel Bragg to evacuate the city on September 7. Bragg was forced to withdraw to northern Georgia, where he concentrated his army at Lafayette and prepared to make a counterattack.

The armies maneuver

Rosecrans left a small force in Chattanooga and moved his army of 62,000 men southward into northern Georgia, believing Bragg was still in retreat. The three Union army corps became widely separated during the movement. Bragg saw his opportunity to strike at Rosecrans and moved west. He failed twice to bring Union forces to battle, however, and Rosecrans, sensing danger, ordered his army to concentrate closer to Chattanooga. Meanwhile, Bragg was reinforced by two divisions

The Union line advances through the forest toward the Confederates at the Battle of Chickamauga.

under James Longstreet from the Army of Northern Virginia, bringing his total strength to 65,000.

As the Union army moved north on September 18, Rosecrans ordered George H. Thomas to position his corps north of Thomas L. Crittenden's corps to prevent Bragg from cutting off the Union army from Chattanooga. Not realizing that Thomas now formed the left flank of the Union army, Bragg crossed his forces over Chickamauga Creek and camped on the night of September 18 after some skirmishing with two Union cavalry brigades. The opposing battle lines were set, but due to the thickly wooded terrain along the creek, neither side was aware of it.

A single Union division initiated the battle on the morning of September 19. It advanced believing that it had

Armies on the battlefield at Chickamauga. The area was a large natural amphitheater. The terrain was mainly flat and covered by thick forest.

trapped a small Confederate force west of Chickamauga Creek. The fighting was confused and inconclusive, with both sides suffering heavy casualties. A late afternoon attack by John Bell Hood's Confederates threatened to split the Union line, but reinforcements plugged the gap at the last moment.

Final day of battle

Rosecrans planned to fight on the defensive the next day and had his men dig trenches for their protection. Bragg planned an all-out attack to force the Union army south, away from Chattanooga and toward destruction.

Initial Confederate attacks on the 20th began four hours late due to poor staff work and made little headway against Thomas's well-situated defensive line on the Union left. At 11:00 A.M. Rosecrans made a critical mistake when he pulled Thomas Wood's division out of the right of his line to plug what he thought was a gap further north. There had been no gap, however, until the movement of Wood's division created one. Fortunately for the Confederates, three of their divisions under Longstreet launched an attack into the gap at precisely the same time. Before Rosecrans could correct his

mistake, the Union's defensive position was shattered. As Longstreet's men came close to cutting his line of communication with Chattanooga, Rosecrans ordered a retreat.

The "Rock of Chickamauga"

Not all Union forces were through fighting. Troops under George H. Thomas made a stand on Snodgrass Hill, a wooded ridge on the northern end of the Union line. In one of the war's most heroic defensive stands Thomas and his force succeeded in holding Bragg at bay as Rosecrans and the bulk of the Union army withdrew into Chattanooga. For his efforts Thomas earned the Medal of Honor and was thereafter known as the "Rock of Chickamauga." In stark contrast to Thomas, Rosecrans was inconsolable as he was carried along into Chattanooga by the wreckage of his army.

Chickamauga was a hollow victory for the Confederates because Bragg was unable to follow it up with the final defeat of the Army of the Cumberland. At a cost of more than 18,000 casualties Bragg could only push Rosecrans back to Chattanooga—he was unable to destroy him or force the surrender of his army by a siege.

Cold Harbor, Battle of

Fought between June 1 and 3, 1864, in central Virginia, the Battle of Cold Harbor took place a month into the Union Army of the Potomac's campaign to attack the Confederate army while moving toward the Confederate capital, Richmond.

The Army of the Potomac was commanded by George G. Meade, but the Union's general-in-chief, Ulysses S. Grant, planned and directed the campaign. In May 1864 Grant tried three times to crush Robert E. Lee's Army of Northern Virginia, at the Wilderness (May 5–6), Spotsylvania (May 10–12), and North Anna River (May 25–26). Each time Lee avoided defeat and withdrew to stand between Grant and Richmond. By May 29 the Army of the Potomac was just 11 miles (18km) northeast of Richmond. Lee had Grant's line of march south covered, but to the east, on his far right flank, lay the Cold Harbor crossroads.

Strategic position

Named for an old tavern, Cold Harbor was only a few miles north of the Chickahominy River, the last natural obstacle between the Union troops and Richmond. If Grant gained control of it, his route south was open once again. His far left flank was at Bethesda Church, several miles north of Cold Harbor. Both Grant and Lee saw that Cold Harbor was a strategically important position and began to concentrate their armies around it.

The Union gained the first success. On May 31 two cavalry divisions under Philip H. Sheridan advanced south from Bethesda Church and drove off Confederate cavalry holding the Cold Harbor crossroads. They were then counterattacked by two divisions of infantry ordered up by Lee. Meade told Sheridan to hold the crossroads "at all hazards" and ordered the Union VI Corps to Cold Harbor to support Sheridan. After an overnight march of nine hours VI Corps relieved the cavalrymen and secured the crossroads by 9:00 A.M on June 1.

Throughout the next two days both armies adjusted their battle lines. By June 2 a 7-mile (11-km) front had formed, extending from Bethesda Church to the Chickahominy River with Cold Harbor in the center. Lee's 58,000-strong army was in position first. Late on June 1 two Union corps

Ulysses S. Grant (standing) examines a map at a gathering of Union commanders at the Army of the Potomac's headquarters at Massaponax Church, Virginia, May 1864.

Battle details

On May 31 Union cavalry captured the Old Cold Harbor crossroads from Confederate cavalry. Two divisions of Confederate infantry counterattacked, but Union reinforcements secured the crossroads by the morning of June 1. There was some fighting on the next two days, but both armies spent much of their time adjusting their battle lines. Early on June 3 Union troops launched their major attack. They suffered losses of about 7,000 troops in just 20 minutes. Stunned, they were unable to continue their assault. Grant arrived on the battlefield at midday and called off the attack. The two sides dug in, and both stayed in position until June 12, when Grant began to withdraw his troops.

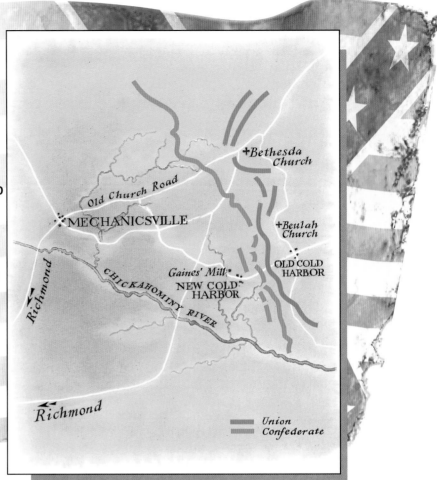

launched a fierce attack but were repulsed. Grant's army of five corps—more than 112,000 men—took longer to maneuver into position, marching on unfamiliar roads in the heat and dust.

Major attack

The major Union attack began at 4:30 A.M. on June 3. It was a disaster from the start. Only three corps at the southern end of the Union line pressed forward. They were met by a devastating crossfire from entrenched Confederate infantry and artillery. One division alone lost more than 1,000 men. A Union captain remembered that "the dreadful storm of lead and iron seemed more like a volcanic blast than a battle." One Confederate general just

called it murder. Within half an hour the assault stopped under the sheer weight of fire, but Grant did not call off the attack until midday, ordering his men to dig in where they could. The two armies confronted each along these battle lines until June 12. Grant later wrote that he regretted that the last attack at Cold Harbor was ever made.

Cold Harbor cost the Union army 7,000 casualties for no gain at all. The Confederates only suffered about 1,500 casualties. Lee had held Grant once again but despite the slaughter could not stop the Union advance. On June 12 Grant began to withdraw his troops and advance once again toward the south, crossing the James River to threaten Petersburg.

Columbia

Columbia, capital of South Carolina, the first state to secede from the Union, was a transportation center and home to many Confederate agencies during the Civil War. Much of the city was destroyed by fire on February 17, 1865.

The chain of events that led to the burning of Columbia began earlier in February 1865, when Union troops under William T. Sherman marched through South Carolina on their way north from Savannah, Georgia.

Union march to Columbia

As in Georgia, the Union troops systematically ripped up railroads and destroyed crops and livestock. Sherman divided his forces in two, making it difficult for the Confederates to effectively oppose the two-pronged Union advance. They were further weakened by their failure to anticipate Sherman's next move.

This came on February 7, when Union troops cut the Augusta–Charleston Railroad near Blackville. The Confederates were forced to retreat across the Edisto River. They then concentrated at Chester and Cheraw, abandoning the central part of South Carolina to Sherman.

Union generals Henry W. Slocum and Oliver O. Howard continued their advance, Slocum toward Lexington, and Howard to Columbia. On February 16 a division of the XV Corps reached Columbia and shelled the State House. The city surrendered almost at once.

The following day, as Union troops entered Columbia, someone set fire to bales of cotton that had been piled in the streets. High winds helped spread the blaze, and over half the city was destroyed before the flames were brought under control.

City destroyed

The Union General Slocum witnessed the damage done to the city and later described the devastion: "Nearly all the public buildings, several churches, an orphan asylum, and many of the residences were destroyed. The city was filled with helpless women and children and invalids, many of who were rendered houseless and homeless in a single night. No sadder scene was presented during the war."

Whether the fire was started by retreating Confederates or by arriving Union troops has remained a matter of controversy. The Union army stayed in Columbia until February 20, when it left to continue its march north.

See also

- Carolina, South
- March to the Sea and the Carolinas Campaign
- Secession

A view of Columbia, South Carolina, after the fire that destroyed large parts of the city on February 17, 1865.

Communications and signals

The Civil War was a period of great improvement in military communications. While both sides still sent written messages by mounted courier, they also used a new visual signaling system and the electric telegraph.

The war was fought over an area of hundreds of square miles by armies that numbered tens of thousands. The country they fought in was often semi-wilderness with few settlements. For the armies to operate effectively in such conditions they needed an efficient signaling system.

Wigwagging

The man who developed the system used during the Civil War was a doctor, Albert J. Myer, who had studied sign language for the deaf. In 1856 he put his knowledge to military use and invented a method of signaling using flags in the daytime and lamps at night. It was known as the wigwag system and was tried out by the U.S. Army on the western frontier before the war. The system was simple but effective. It was based on two separate signal movements of either the flag or lamp, which stood for the numbers 1 and 2 (see diagram below). Different combinations of these two signals identified letters, whole phrases, or numbers. A pause signaled the end of one letter and the beginning of the next. A third signal movement (3) marked the end of each word.

Wigwagging messages was slow— three words per minute—but the signals could be sent 20 miles (32km) on a clear day. The system became a prominent feature of Civil War communications and proved its value time and time again. On the battlefield at Allatoona, Georgia, in October 1864, for example, the Union army used wigwagging to call in reinforcements.

In June 1860 Myer was given a major's commission and appointed Signal Officer of the Union army. After

Civil War signalmen sent messages by making simple motions with a flag. Each motion begins and ends with the flag held above the head. All the letters of the alphabet can be made with combinations of motions 1 and 2. For example, "11" is "A" and "1221" is "B." Motion 3 signals the end of each word, "33" the end of a sentence, and "333" the end of the message.

1   2   3

the war broke out in April 1861, Myer set up the Signal Camp of Instruction at Georgetown, Washington, D.C. Myer's work was only semiofficial, and the Union signal service remained in a disorganized state until the federal government established the U.S. Army Signal Corps in August 1864.

U.S. Army Signal Corps

The Signal Corps consisted of 167 officers, 84 noncommissioned officers (NCOs), and 1,266 privates, all commanded by a colonel. Each army and corps headquarters in the field had a signal department. The department was commanded by a captain who ran up to 20 signal parties, each led by a lieutenant in charge of a sergeant and four privates. By 1865 the corps had grown to 300 officers and 2,500 men.

CODE-BREAKING

Both the Union and Confederate armies used the same signaling system at the beginning of the Civil War. This created serious problems because confidential messages from one side could be read by the other. The problem was only solved by sending messages in code (using words with secret meanings) or cipher (scrambled messages). This led to a code-breaking war as teams of cryptanalysts (code-breakers) on both sides worked to decipher the messages sent and received by the enemy. The Confederate Signal Bureau expanded this secret area of its work during the war and took responsibility for the Confederacy's spy networks, which were run by its secret service division.

Confederate Army Signal Bureau

The Confederates also employed Myer's wigwagging system and were the first to use it in battle. By the summer of 1861 Captain Edward P. Alexander, who had been an assistant of Myer's on the frontier, was attached to the staff of Pierre G.T. Beauregard's army at Manassas to organize a series of signal posts. The system was fully operational for the first time at the First Battle of Bull Run on July 21. It gave the warning of a Union flanking march, saving the Confederates and paving the way for their victory later in the day.

The Confederate Army Signal Bureau was established in April 1862. It was attached to the Adjutant and Inspector General's Department in Richmond and commanded by a major with 30 officers and 10 sergeants. There were no private

A Union signal tower on Elk Mountain, overlooking the battlefield of Antietam, Maryland, in September 1862. Signalmen had to send messages from a prominent and visible position, which made them vulnerable to enemy snipers.

soldiers, since they were detailed from the line of the army when they were needed. Each army division and cavalry brigade was assigned its own signal squad of five privates commanded by a sergeant or lieutenant.

Signaling equipment

The wigwag signal flags were large and designed to be clearly visible by powerful telescopes over long distances. The most common types were a white flag with a red square in the middle (for

use at twilight) and a red flag with a white square (for broad daylight). In winter signalmen often used black flags because they showed up against the snow. At night they used colored lamps. Signals could also be sent using rockets and heavy brass signal pistols, which ignited charges of gunpowder.

Signal posts

To transmit a message along an army's battle line, which could extend up to 6 miles (10km), it was necessary to set up a series of signal posts within sight of one another, each manned by an officer or NCO who read off the message and an enlisted man who worked the flag or lamp. On campaign these posts were on high ground or even in tall trees. During the Siege of Petersburg, Virginia, in 1864–1865 Union troops occupied their trench lines for such a length of time that the army built wooden signal towers, some up to 140 feet (43m) tall.

Signal posts were often in exposed positions, and that made a signalman's work very dangerous. Although he was not classed as a combat soldier, he was a prime target for sharpshooters and artillery batteries that hoped to disrupt the enemy's communications by disabling a signal post. One Union signal tower was shot at more than 250 times by Confederate artillery during a single day of the Petersburg siege.

The electric telegraph

The telegraph, which had been developed in the 1840s, was an important method of communication during the war. By 1861 the United States had 50,000 miles (80,000km) of telegraph wire crisscrossing the country, providing the fastest method of

A soldier from the Union Corps of Engineers repairs a telegraph wire. The telegraph allowed generals in the field to communicate quickly with the government in Washington.

communication yet achieved. The Union government recognized immediately that the telegraph could be a war-winning technology and acted swiftly to gain control of it. In April 1861 the Union government seized all the commercial telegraph systems around Washington, D.C., and in early 1862 the War Department took over all private lines and railroad telegraphs.

To run the system and extend it to keep pace with the advancing Union armies, the Military Telegraph Corps was set up in November 1861. It was a separate organization from the Signal Corps and was run directly from the War Department in Washington. Army commanders had no control over it, which caused some friction between the telegraphers and Signal Corps officers. The job the telegraphers did, however, was vital in waging war on a continental scale. By 1865 they had established over 15,000 miles (24,000km) of new lines and sent and received 750,000 messages a year.

The Confederates, who lacked the resources of the Union, did not have a separate telegraph corps. Instead, the Signal Bureau worked with privately owned telegraph companies to provide the army with a basic system. The Confederates also used the Union's telegraph system for their own benefit. Partisan cavalry working behind the lines became skilled at tapping into the system to read messages or send false information to Union commanders.

ABOVE THE WHITE HOUSE

The telegraph was used to send messages from one of the war's most interesting innovations, the hydrogen balloon. Thaddeus S.C. Lowe, an "aeronaut," as balloonists were called, traveled to Washington in June 1861. He intended to sell to the War Department his idea for a Union Balloon Corps to observe Confederate troop positions from the air. Lowe linked his balloon *Enterprise* to the telegraph system and ascended 1,000 feet (305m) above the White House. Lowe then sent President Lincoln a telegram from his excellent vantage point: "The city, with its girdle of encampments, presents a superb scene."

It was a brilliant piece of public relations, and the government established a Union Balloon Corps that year. Lowe received funding for seven new balloons, two of which, the *Constitution* and *Intrepid*, were used during George B. McClellan's Peninsular Campaign of 1862.

The Union Balloon Corps prepares to launch a hydrogen balloon. Telegrams could be sent by wire from the air.

41

Confederate army

The Confederacy began to organize its armies barely a month before the Civil War broke out in April 1861. The regular army was soon dwarfed by the provisional Confederate army, made up of 12-month militiamen and volunteers.

The Confederacy started the war with very little in the way of armed forces. State militias were organized by and remained within their home state. As each state seceded and declared itself an independent entity, its own army might emerge.

The prewar South had a strong military tradition, with three military colleges—the Virginia Military Institute, the Citadel in Charleston, South Carolina, and what later became Louisiana State University, as well as a great many other military schools. This meant that the Confederacy had a great supply of junior officers for the lower levels of command. The North, on the other hand, had only the U.S. Military Academy at West Point. West Point supplied most of the senior officers in the U.S. Army. When the war began, however, the Confederacy attracted the services of about the same number of U.S. Army officers and West Point graduates as did the Union.

Field forces

The term "army" applies not only to the entire Confederate force but also to individual field forces. There were at least 23 separate Confederate armies during the war, though not all at the same time. The main Confederate army was the Army of Northern Virginia, commanded for most of the war by Robert E. Lee. It served principally in the eastern theater (east of the Appalachian Mountains). The main army in the western theater (between the Appalachians and the Mississippi River) was the Army of Tennessee.

The first Confederate army was the Army of South Carolina, which confronted the Union forces at Fort Sumter in April 1861 at the start of the war. It was originally a state force made up of various militia units, volunteers, and cadets from the Citadel. President Jefferson Davis appointed Pierre G.T. Beauregard as the Confederacy's first brigadier general and sent him to Charleston. Beauregard took governmental control of the Army of South Carolina, which became the Confederates' first national force.

Three battle-hardened Confederate soldiers, who were taken prisoner during the Battle of Gettysburg, Pennsylvania (July 1–3, 1863).

CONFEDERATE GENERALS

Unlike the Union, which had only two ranks of generals — brigadier and major generals (one star and two star)—the Confederacy had four: brigadier general, major general, lieutenant general, and (full) general.

The leading Confederate generals were Samuel Cooper, Albert S. Johnston, Robert E. Lee, Joseph E. Johnston, and Pierre G.T. Beauregard. John Bell Hood was also named a full general, but the promotion was revoked after his

failure in command. Of these senior officers both Joseph E. Johnston and Beauregard were alienated from Jefferson Davis for several reasons. Johnston was angry that his appointment as full general dated from July 1861, making him only the fourth-ranking general, when he had been senior brigadier general in the U.S. Army before the war.

A montage of the generals of the Confederate armies. The most famous, Robert E. Lee, is at the front in civilian dress.

The Confederates typically named their armies for states or regions. Like the Union, the Confederacy divided its territory into military departments. However, the Confederates placed much more emphasis on the system, which proved to be awkward and ultimately unsatisfactory. A military department was a large administrative area covering one or more states. Each department had a commander, who was in theory also the commander of any field army in his area. However, the system worked poorly because the responsibilities of the department commander were not clearly defined in relation to the commanders of the

armies. As a result, troops were often not positioned near enemy units, and troops in any given department did not cooperate with those in the areas of greatest need.

Jefferson's errors

The Confederacy was fortunate to get its abler men into key positions at the start of the war. This advantage was lost, however, by President Davis, who made three key errors. He raised his classmate and friend, Leonidas Polk, to the rank of general. He never performed very satisfactorily. Despite this, he was allowed to stay in his post until his death in 1864.

Confederate Private Thomas Taylor of the 8th Louisiana Infantry, in full kit, armed with a musket.

Davis also retained faith for too long in Braxton Bragg, who had impressed him early in the war, but who proved inadequate as a highly placed combat commander. When Davis finally removed Bragg from field command, he made him a principal military adviser. Last, Davis made a mistake in giving command of an army to John Bell Hood, who had been promoted beyond his competence.

Army organization

The largest component in the armies of both sides was the corps, a system adopted from the French army (see box.) There were typically two or three corps in a Confederate army, while a Union army had seven or eight smaller corps. Confederate units were often named for their commanders or former commanders, which could be confusing when the commander was transferred.

RAGGED CONFEDERATES

Major General E. M. Law described the Confederate Army of Northern Virginia in spring 1865:

"The army had ... never been so scantily supplied with food and clothing. The equipment as to arms was well enough for men who knew how to use them, but commissary and quartermasters' supplies were lamentably deficient. A new pair of shoes or an overcoat was a luxury and and full rations would have astonished the stomachs of Lee's ragged Confederates. But they took their privations cheerfully and complaints were seldom heard.

"I have often heard expressions of surprise that these ragged, barefooted, half-starved men would fight at all. But the very fact that they remained with their colors through such privations and hardships was sufficient to prove that they would be dangerous foes to encounter upon the line of battle. The morale of the army at this time was excellent."

The Confederates placed regiments from the same state in the same brigades whenever possible, which raised morale and allowed brigades to develop a distinct identity. Famous examples include Hood's Texas brigade of Lee's Army of Northern Virginia and the 1st Kentucky (Orphan) brigade of the Army of Tennessee.

Armies on both sides were organized around the infantry. Civil War battles, with few exceptions, principally involved infantry fighting with rifled muskets, supported by the cavalry and artillery. The Confederate cavalry was a great strength: It completely outclassed the Union cavalry, at least in the first two years. But the Confederacy was at a disadvantage regarding weapons and ammunition, partly because it had fewer manufacturing facilities.

Quality of soldiers

More Southerners at the outset were comfortable with outdoor life, just as they were better horsemen. However, Northern soldiers gradually caught up. More important was the fact that many more Northern soldiers had some kind of occupational training, and far more had been exposed to typical childhood diseases. Huge numbers of Southerners succumbed to measles, including an entire garrison at Camp Moore, a Louisiana training facility.

Morale, religion, and thoughts of family back home were very important for the soldiers. Confederate morale was often good despite difficult conditions. Historians still debate how much the soldiers were motivated by commitment to a cause. Some consider ideology to have been very important, while others believe it had little effect. The regiment and brigade structure was certainly very significant—much of the soldiers' motivation came from their

commitment to their comrades in arms. The Confederacy's lack of resources badly affected the army. Soldiers were often hampered by a lack of equipment, clothing—especially boots and shoes—and food (see box opposite). Despite such difficulties, the Southerners hung in doggedly for a remarkably long time.

Confederate 3rd State Infantry on parade in Arkansas, June 1861.

TYPICAL ARMY STRUCTURE

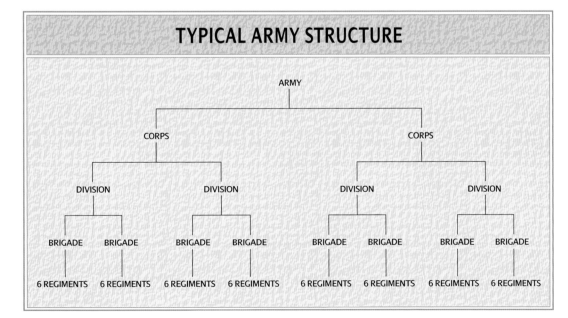

See also

- Artillery
- Cavalry
- Desertion
- Discipline, military
- Infantry tactics
- Morale
- Recruitment
- Soldier life
- Strategy and tactics
- Training
- Uniforms
- Union army
- Weapons and firearms

Confederate government

No sooner had the Confederate government been established than it went to war. Jefferson Davis's administration, just like Lincoln's in the North, was criticized for harsh wartime measures that trampled individual rights.

The Confederate government first met in the state capitol at Montgomery, Alabama (pictured above). The government then moved to Richmond, Virginia, in May 1861, creating a flood of people and jobs that transformed the city.

On February 4, 1861, delegates from South Carolina, Georgia, Florida, Alabama, Mississippi, Louisiana, and Texas convened at Montgomery, Alabama. These were the seven states of the lower South that had seceded from the United States. The purpose of the convention was to create a new nation and government.

A swift pace

Within days the delegates had drawn up and approved a provisional constitution, elected a president and vice president, and established themselves as a provisional congress.

On February 18 Jefferson Davis was inaugurated as the first president of the Confederate States of America. The appointment applied until elections could be held in November.

The speed with which the Confederacy was established reflected the urgency of the situation. In the Union President Buchanan's term was drawing to a close, with President-elect Lincoln due to be inaugurated on March 4. The new Confederacy expected war and began to organize its defenses. It was of critical importance for the seceded states to persuade the slave-holding states in the upper South to join them. By establishing the Confederacy with a confident flourish, they hoped to encourage more states to secede. The Confederacy also hoped to gain recognition of its nationhood from Britain and France. This goal was never achieved despite a number of Confederate diplomatic missions that went to Europe during the war years.

Drafting a constitution

The new Confederate constitution mirrored the U.S. Constitution in structure, but it was ambiguous about how power was to be divided between the new federal government and the states (see box opposite). It also differed, pointedly, on the matter of slavery. It said that the congress could make no laws "denying or impairing the

THE CONFEDERATE CONSTITUTION

The Confederate constitution had a very familiar look to it, since most of it was copied word for word from the U.S. Constitution of 1787. The Confederacy claimed to be acting in accordance with the principles laid down by the Founders. Like the Constitution of 1787, it tried to balance states' rights with federal power. The doctrine of states' rights was sacred to Confederates; on it they had based their right to secede from the Union. So the preamble to the constitution had a clause claiming that each state was acting in its "sovereign and independent character." However, the constitution went on to say that the intention was "to form a permanent government." This implied that by signing up to the Confederacy, the states accepted that they could never secede from it as they had just done from the United States. The Confederacy never created a supreme court to ensure that new laws and all legislative decisions followed the letter of its new constitution. The Confederate constitution also appeared to strengthen the executive branch of the government by granting the president a six-year term. However, it stipulated one term only. The United States eventually followed this lead by limiting the number of terms a president could serve.

right of property in negro slaves." Slavery was to be legal everywhere in the Confederacy for all time. The foreign slave trade, however, which had been outlawed by the United States in 1807, and which many Southerners wanted to see reopened, was prohibited on practical grounds. It would alienate Britain, which was the principal market for Southern cotton. It would also antagonize the upper South, which had a surplus of slaves and enjoyed a monopoly on exporting them to the lower South, where the demand in the cotton fields was unrelenting.

The new president

The delegates were also careful to choose a moderate as their president. Jefferson Davis was a compromise choice but, at first glance, an inspired one. He looked like a president—a real Southern gentleman, tall and dignified in his bearing. More to the point, Davis's credentials were impressive. The Mississippi planter was a graduate of the U.S. Military Academy at West Point and had distinguished himself in the Mexican War. He was an experienced senator and had served as secretary of war under President Franklin Pierce in the 1850s. Davis had played a leading role as a Southern Democrat in standing up for Southern rights; but while he supported secession he had a reputation for moderation. This, it was felt, would make him acceptable in the eyes of the rest of the world. So Davis was elected unanimously on February 9.

A cartoon showing the leaders of the six Southern states that had seceded by January 1861. Each sits on his state's source of wealth—the South Carolina governor sits on a slave; Jefferson Davis of Mississippi (third from right) sits on a cotton bale.

Alexander H. Stephens of Georgia—a tiny figure weighing less than 100 pounds (45 kg)—was chosen as vice president. Stephens missed out on the presidency in part because he had stuck to the Union until the last minute and was therefore far too much of a moderate for the ardent secessionists or "fire-eaters" among the delegates.

Taking power

Jefferson Davis made his first public appearance as president to a cheering crowd in Montgomery on February 18. One of the reception party proclaimed "the man and the hour have met." Davis then made a warlike speech in which he said that "The South is determined to maintain her position, and make all who oppose her smell Southern powder and feel Southern steel!"

That same month Davis sent a peace commission to Washington, but his priority was to mobilize for war with the Union. When Lincoln sent warships to resupply Fort Sumter, South Carolina, in April, Davis ordered the bombing of the fort. With the outbreak of war Virginia, North Carolina, Tennessee, and Arkansas made the decision to secede and join the Confederacy. The slave states of Delaware, Maryland, Kentucky, and Missouri, however, remained in the Union. Virginia's capital, Richmond, was named the new capital of the expanded Confederacy.

A war government

Early Confederate military successes increased Southern optimism about the outcome of the conflict, and Davis and his administration basked in public approval—he was unopposed as president in the November election.

By the spring of 1862 this heady enthusiasm was over. The swelling Union armies and the Union navy were poised to attack on every front, while the Confederate army was too small to defend the nation's long borders. The initial surge of volunteers slowed to a trickle. Critics of the government began to make their voices heard. Many wanted the government to conduct the war with more energy. One Confederate general advocated total war in which "the whole population and the whole production … are to be put on a war footing."

Robert E. Lee, Davis's military adviser, was in no doubt that to win the war, the government in Richmond had to coerce men into the army. Davis moved in this direction decisively and to the dismay of many. He stunned the congress by asking it to pass a law conscripting all able-bodied

The Great Seal of the Confederacy bore the nation's motto Deo Vindice, *meaning "God will vindicate." The seal arrived in Richmond just before the city was evacuated in April 1865, and the Confederate authorities left it behind when they fled.*

THE CABINET

President Davis chose his first cabinet swiftly, ensuring that all the original Confederate states were represented. Robert Toombs of Georgia (a disappointed candidate for the presidency) became secretary of state. Christopher G. Memminger of South Carolina was secretary of the treasury, and Leroy Pope Walker, an Alabamian, secretary of war. The constitution allowed Davis great power to appoint secretaries at will, and he used cabinet jobs as political weapons or rewards, often to the frustration of congress. In all, 14 men held cabinet positions. Of them six were imprisoned after the war, four were not arrested, and four fled the country.

individual and state liberties—the very matter that had provoked secession in the first place. Political opponents were plentiful but not united, since political parties were banned in the Confederacy. Individuals therefore took the lead in opposing the administration. Joseph Brown, governor of Georgia, fought the government over martial law, which suspended the right to trial, the employment of Georgia troops far from their home state, and uneven tax

A poster of 1864 showing the most influential men in the Confederate government. President Davis is shown in the center with Vice President Stephens above him.

men between the age of 18 and 35 into the Confederate forces for at least three years. Davis got his way, and in April 1862 the first draft law ever imposed in America was passed. Conscription is always unpopular, but it was hated for the unfair way in which it was applied in the Confederacy. Confederate and state civil officials were exempt, for example, while rich men were able to buy their way out of the draft by hiring a substitute.

Davis also pressured the Confederate Congress into accepting martial law to deal with civilian unrest and to provide money to invest in war industries that were woefully lacking in the South.

Fierce opposition

Davis's administration was severely criticized for increasing the power of central government at the expense of

The flight of President Jefferson Davis and his cabinet following the Union capture of Richmond on April 2, 1865. They attempted to run a government in exile until May 2.

distribution between the states. He also undermined the draft by appointing huge numbers of exempt civil servants.

Brown, like others, believed that his opposition would prevent the sort of government established by Davis from continuing after the South had won its independence. Alexander H. Stephens was also tenacious in opposing Davis in all matters where he saw a threat to states' rights. To the vice president and many others the argument put forward by Davis that winning the war had to be an absolute priority was flawed. Liberty, for Stephens, was the priority because "Our liberties, once lost, may be lost forever." As the war ground on, Davis came under increasingly fierce fire from such critics. He was derisively nicknamed "King Jeff the First."

Desperate measures

The Confederate government also interfered more and more in economic life as the war went against it, and with increasing desperation. The military was authorized to seize food and raw materials and to direct slave labor to help the war effort. The War Department set up factories to manufacture weapons and ammunition and other tools of war. The government also used taxes to create an industrial base that was lacking at the outset of the war. Some measures were taken too late to help the war effort. For example, the government did not commandeer railroads until 1865.

By the fall of 1864 the Confederacy was facing defeat, and Davis took one final gamble. He decided that the Confederacy's only hope lay in using black Southerners as soldiers. He accepted that such a policy could never work while the blacks remained slaves, so he proposed freeing and arming the slaves. Davis's proposal caused an uproar. He managed to force it through congress in the spring of 1865, shortly before events on the battlefield made it irrelevant. On April 9 Lee surrendered to Grant at Appomattox, while Davis had already fled Richmond. Davis was captured a month later in Georgia.

Confederate navy

At the outbreak of war the Confederate states had few ships or shipyards and little naval tradition. They tried to make up for this with resourcefulness and several innovations such as the sea mine (then called the torpedo.)

The Confederacy's first and only secretary of the navy, Stephen R. Mallory, faced a difficult task. When his Department of the Navy came into being in February 1861, Mallory had almost no vessels under his control and only a single naval facility—little more than a coaling station—confiscated from the U.S. Navy at Pensacola, Florida. Virginia's secession two months later brought the important Norfolk naval yard into Confederate hands, but only after evacuating Union forces had significantly damaged it. Of the 1,457 officers of the prewar U.S. Navy only 237 cast their lot with the Confederacy.

Mallory, an energetic, forceful administrator, was able to fashion from this unpromising start a navy that played a respectable role throughout the conflict. Outgunned by the Union navy, Mallory followed a traditional American naval strategy based on coastal defense and commerce raiding. Once the Union blockade of Southern ports began to take effect, he added an emphasis on blockade-running.

The ironclads

Unable to compete with the enemy on numerical terms, Mallory substituted innovation for quantity, particularly in the area of ironclad warships. The 1860s were a time of transition in naval technology. None of the world's navies had yet settled on a warship design that would make the best use of the new rifled naval cannon, steam propulsion, and armor plating. The British and French had only two effective ironclad warships; the Union navy had none. Here, then, was one area in which the Confederacy could compete on equal terms. During the course of the war the

A Confederate ironclad, one of the remarkable range of vessels deployed in the Civil War. Several were at the cutting edge of naval technology. They carried a variety of weapons, from conventional cannons to innovative rams and "spar torpedoes"— explosive charges attached to long poles.

The Confederate ironclad CSS Virginia *rammed and sank the 24-gun wooden frigate USS* Cumberland *in the Battle of Hampton Roads, Virginia, on March 8, 1862. The engagement showed that wooden ships were no match for the new ironclads.*

Confederate navy began construction of nearly 50 ironclads, of which 22 were actually put into commission.

The CSS *Virginia*

By far the most famous ironclad was the CSS *Virginia*. This ship was adapted from the hulk of the frigate USS *Merrimack*, which had been only partly destroyed when the Norfolk naval yard was abandoned by Union forces. The new ironclad rode so low in the water that it looked like the roof of a floating barn. It mounted ten 11-inch (25-cm) cannons and an iron ram on the bow below the waterline.

The *Virginia* briefly struck terror in Union hearts. During its maiden voyage on March 8, 1862, it steamed from Norfolk into Hampton Roads, Virginia, where it rammed and sank one Union frigate, destroyed another with gunfire, and ran a third warship aground before retiring for the night. The next day it steamed forth to wreak further havoc, only to be confronted by an oddly shaped vessel. It was the USS *Monitor*, the Union's answer to the *Virginia*. The Union had found out about the

Confederacy's new ship and had built an ironclad of its own. The *Monitor* successfully neutralized the *Virginia*; but even if it had failed to do so, it is difficult to see how much more damage the Confederate ironclad could inflict. The *Virginia* was too unseaworthy to sail beyond the protected waters of Hampton Roads and drew too much water to steam up to the Potomac River and Washington, D.C., or for that matter, to withdraw up the James River estuary to guard Richmond. Just two months after its duel with the *Monitor* the *Virginia* had to be scuttled to prevent its capture as Union ground troops approached Norfolk.

The *Virginia* epitomized the problems of Confederate ironclads. All too often they were slow, unwieldy, and suffered from many mechanical defects. The best that could be said of them is that they complicated the Union's task of capturing coastal areas and ports.

Coastal defenses

To defend their ports, the Confederates made great use of sea mines (then called torpedoes), which were explosive charges anchored in shipping channels. They were powerful enough to damage or sink any ship that came into contact with them. Union Admiral David G. Farragut's famous cry "Damn the torpedoes! Go ahead!" at the Battle of Mobile Bay in August 1864 was made just after he witnessed one of his ships sunk by such a torpedo.

A torpedo could also be deployed by being attached to a long spar mounted on a small, fast, unarmored vessel. The spar would strike an enemy vessel, and the torpedo would explode, but the torpedo boat itself usually survived with little or no damage.

The most famous example of such a torpedo boat was also the most unusual: the CSS *Hunley*, a submersible vessel powered by a crew of eight, which attempted to destroy part of the Union fleet blockading the harbor of Charleston, South Carolina. On the night of February 17, 1864, the *Hunley* successfully rammed a spar torpedo into the side of the sloop of war USS *Housatonic*. The *Housatonic* sank in shallow water. However, it lost only five men, while the entire crew of the *Hunley* perished in the attack.

Blockade-runners and commerce raiders

To evade the Union naval blockade of Southern ports, the Confederacy took advantage of blockade-runners—fast, steam-driven vessels often specifically designed to outrun patrol ships. Many were privately owned. But because the captains of such vessels preferred to carry cargos of luxury goods, the Confederate navy commissioned 43 of its own blockade-runners to ensure that enough arms, ammunition, and other military essentials got through to sustain the war effort.

The Confederacy briefly tried using privateers. Privateering was a kind of legalized piracy in which a government gave private vessels letters of marque permitting them to capture enemy shipping. The practice had once been very profitable, but most European powers had disowned it. As the Union blockade became more effective, captains found it too difficult to bring captured prizes into Southern ports, which was the only way to make privateering pay. For that reason the Confederacy turned increasingly to commerce raiders with regular naval crews that were designed to destroy, not capture, enemy merchantmen.

The Confederate commerce raiders achieved great notoriety and in some respects great effectiveness. Many commerce raiders were built in England, secretly commissioned by a Confederate agent in London, James Bulloch. (He also tried to get ironclads built in Britain but was blocked by the British government.) Commerce raiders sank a large number of Union merchantmen, forced hundreds more to seek refuge by reregistering under

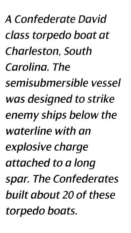

A Confederate David class torpedo boat at Charleston, South Carolina. The semisubmersible vessel was designed to strike enemy ships below the waterline with an explosive charge attached to a long spar. The Confederates built about 20 of these torpedo boats.

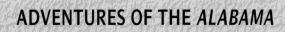

ADVENTURES OF THE *ALABAMA*

The greatest Southern commerce raider was the CSS *Alabama* (*below*), commanded by Captain Raphael Semmes. Built in England, the *Alabama* mounted eight guns and could reach a speed of more than 13 knots under steam. Starting in August 1862, it destroyed 68 Union vessels in 22 months—without injuring the crews. The sailors boarded the enemy merchantmen and took their seamen prisoner before destroying the vessels. When the *Alabama* grew too crowded, Semmes would designate the next captured merchantman a "cartel ship," place the prisoners on board, and let them sail to the nearest port. In that way he accomplished his mission without bloodshed.

The *Alabama*'s colorful career lasted until June 1864, when the Union frigate USS *Kearsarge* cornered the raider in the port of Cherbourg, France. The *Kearsarge* waited outside the port, barring escape. The *Alabama* came forth to fight but was sunk in a spirited one-hour engagement. Semmes himself went over the side. He was picked up by the *Deerhound*, a yacht filled with admiring sightseers, who helped him escape capture by taking him to England.

neutral flags, and sent insurance premiums soaring. The commerce raider CSS *Shenandoah*, for example, managed to cripple the New England whaling fleet in the Bering Sea— although it achieved this in June 1865, unaware that the war was over.

Effectiveness of the navy

Although Mallory did a superb job of creating a navy—he even set up a naval academy to train new officers—it must be questioned whether that navy achieved results worth even the relatively slender resources spent on it.

The ironclad program produced several formidable vessels, but they usually failed to prevent Union warships from capturing a Southern port when they mounted a major effort to do so. Land fortifications, not armored vessels, seemed the most effective way to defend Southern harbors. The commerce raiders, for their part, did considerable damage, but never enough to deflate the North's will to continue the war. Considering the vast amount of commerce carried by Northern ships, the raiders were really little more than a nuisance.

Connecticut

Connecticut played a leading role in the Union war effort. Many of the Union's small arms and much of its ammunition were manufactured in the state, which also contributed more than 50,000 men to the Union armed forces.

Historically Connecticut was predominantly liberal. Most inhabitants were opposed to slavery, which was abolished in the state in 1848. The Republican Party, which was founded in 1854, soon attracted a wide following in Connecticut because of its opposition to the spread of slavery in the western territories.

Gideon Welles

One of the most important early Republican leaders in the state was Gideon Welles (1802–1878). A former editor of the *Hartford Times*, Welles served as a Democrat in the Connecticut legislature from 1827 to 1835. He left the Democratic Party because he disagreed with its proslavery stance. Welles helped organize the new Republican Party and in 1854 founded the *Hartford Evening Press*, one of the first Republican newspapers in the United States.

In 1861 Welles was appointed secretary of the navy by the new president, Abraham Lincoln. He quickly achieved the remarkable feat of building an adequate navy from the poorly equipped prewar force. Under Welles' direction Union warships enforced the blockade of Confederate ports to starve the South of vital supplies. He also established a fleet of gunboats and ironclads to patrol the Mississippi River.

William A. Buckingham

In 1858 William A. Buckingham, a Republican, was elected governor of Connecticut, a position he held throughout the Civil War. He was a strong supporter of both the war and the Lincoln administration, and urged a rapid end to slavery. In 1863 Buckingham was challenged by Thomas H. Seymour, a veteran Democrat and former governor. Seymour's campaign drew attention to the faults of the Lincoln administration, especially its violations of civil liberties, its incompetent military leadership, and the excessive cost and waste of the war. However, Buckingham rallied the pro-Union antislavery forces

William A. Buckingham was the governor of Connecticut during the Civil War. He was called "Connecticut's Lincoln" because of his strong leadership and loyalty to the preservation of the Union.

COLT FACTORY

Samuel Colt, a native of Hartford, Connecticut, patented a repeating pistol in 1835–1836. It had a cartridge cylinder that was revolved by cocking a hammer. The new gun was slow to gain popularity, and Colt's first business in New Jersey failed. However, reports of the pistol's effectiveness against Native Americans in Florida and Texas resulted in the U.S. government ordering 1,000 revolvers for use in the Mexican War in 1847. Two years later Colt established a factory in his hometown, and his business began to flourish. In 1855 he built the largest private arms factory in the world on the Connecticut River in Hartford. When the Civil War broke out, Colt quickly increased the capacity of his factory, which went on producing at full tilt until it was temporarily put out of action by a serious fire in February 1864. His revolving-breech pistol became so popular that the word Colt was sometimes used as a general term for revolver.

The 1851 Colt Model .36 caliber was a popular revolver in the Civil War.

to rout the Democrats in the election. By the time of the 1864 elections the situation was very different. Union commander William T. Sherman was sweeping through the lower South, and Ulysses S. Grant was well on his way to the Confederate capital of Richmond, Virginia. These developments helped the Republicans retain control of Connecticut, which again voted for Lincoln by a landslide.

Contribution to the war

Both economically and militarily, Connecticut played a large part in the Union victory. Within three days of Fort Sumter's surrender in April 1861 Connecticut volunteers had formed one regiment, and in another three weeks there were five more. Many of the soldiers were Irish, German, Scottish, and Scandinavian immigrants. Two African American Connecticut regiments also served with distinction. In all, Connecticut sent between 55,000 and 57,000 men to the Civil War in 30 infantry units, one of cavalry, and two of heavy artillery, plus three battalions of light artillery. The state also contributed 250 officers and 2,500 men to the Union navy.

Connecticut units took part in every major battle and campaign of the Civil War, notably Antietam and Gettysburg, in which they suffered heavy losses. By the end of the war 20,000 Connecticut participants were casualties.

Arms factories

Connecticut's main contribution to the war effort was the production of munitions. The firms and factories of the state turned out 1,000 rifles a month early in the war and doubled that figure by 1864. The leading company was that of Samuel Colt (see box). The other leading arms manufacturers in Connecticut were Christian Sharps' Rifle Company and the Norfolk Arms Company.

Powder, cartridges, clothing, and wagons were also produced in great quantities in the state. Private civilians banded together to provide aid and supplies to men at the front and in hospitals. Vessels for the Union navy were built at the shipyards in Mystic.

After the Civil War industry in Connecticut continued to expand. The state's cities grew rapidly, and large numbers of immigrants arrived from Europe and Canada to work in the growing businesses.

Contrabands

Slaves who managed to escape from their masters in the Confederate states and reach the protection of the Union armies during the Civil War were called contrabands. They provided a large workforce to help the Union war effort.

At the start of the Civil War the first opportunity for slaves to make a bid for freedom came when Union General Benjamin F. Butler took command of Fort Monroe on the Virginia peninsula in May 1861. Almost at once groups of fugitive slaves began to arrive at the fort asking Butler to set them free. There was no official government policy, so Butler took matters into his own hands.

Butler's decision

Under the terms of the 1850 Fugitive Slave Act all runaway slaves were meant to be returned to their masters. However, Butler, who was a radical Republican politician and abolitionist, refused to surrender the people who had sought refuge in the fort. He argued that since Virginia claimed to be part of a foreign country—the Confederacy—the law did not apply in that state. He declared the slaves to be "contraband of war," invoking an international law of war that allowed the confiscation of any enemy property that might be used to continue the conflict. Butler put the "contrabands," as they were named from then on, to work in his army, unloading provisions and building roads and fortifications.

Butler had made an important political decision. He had established that the question of slavery was central to the Civil War. His initiative was

regarded with suspicion in the North since many considered the purpose of the war to be preserving the Union. Angering Virginia was likely to deepen and prolong divisions.

Government policy

As Union troops moved into Confederate territory, the number of fugitive slaves grew, but the Union remained unsure about what to do with them. In summer 1861 Union troops were still returning many runaway slaves to their owners, especially in the West. The officers responsible justified their actions by saying that they had no system to care for fugitives.

Contrabands at Cobbs Mill, Virginia, in 1864. Many contrabands contributed to the Union war effort by working as laborers in the army.

In August 1861 Congress adopted Butler's initiative and codified policy in the Confiscation Act. All fugitive slaves who had been used in the Confederate cause were to be considered a prize of war. Their former masters would have no lawful claim to them. They were not given their freedom but used to contribute to the Union war effort

Some Union commanders freed slaves in areas they controlled, notably John C. Frémont in Missouri and David Hunter in South Carolina. These individual actions were countermanded by President Lincoln, who wanted the process of emancipation to be decided and agreed on by Congress.

A second Confiscation Act of July 1862 declared the contrabands to be free. The Militia Act of the same month authorized them to be used in "any military or naval service," opening the way for blacks to become soldiers.

Treatment of contrabands

Union commanders set up camps for the contrabands and integrated them into the Union war effort. Some worked as fieldhands, others as laborers, cooks, and servants for the army.

The treatment of contrabands varied widely depending on whose control they fell under. In December 1862

Rufus Saxton, then commanding the Department of the South, allowed contrabands to settle on abandoned lands. He gave them 2 acres (0.8ha) of land each and tools to plant crops for their own use. In return, they had to produce cotton for government use.

In some cases superintendents were appointed to oversee the contrabands' welfare, and private relief associations provided additional supplies and helped with their education. On the other hand, William T. Sherman treated the thousands of contrabands who flocked to the Union army on his March to the Sea in 1864 with brutal disregard.

In general the Union army failed to assimilate the huge influx of contrabands. Camps were overcrowded and unhealthy, and many died from disease, exposure, and starvation. One camp official reported a 25 percent mortality rate over two years.

In January 1863 the Emancipation Proclamation declared all slaves in the Confederate states free, and by the spring of that year the Union was actively recruiting large numbers of blacks to serve as soldiers and sailors. On March 3, 1865, Congress set up the Freedmen's Bureau to help former slaves and their families establish themselves in their new lives.

A contraband camp in Richmond, Virginia, in 1865. The camps were often overcrowded and unhealthy.

Copperheads

During the war the Democratic Party in the North was deeply divided. War Democrats supported President Abraham Lincoln's policies, while Peace Democrats—nicknamed Copperheads—opposed the conduct of the war.

In July 1861 the *New York Tribune* coined the nickname "Copperhead" to liken antiwar Democrats to the poisonous snake of that name. By 1863 the term was being widely used, and some Peace Democrats proudly accepted the label. They wore copper pennies depicting the Goddess of Liberty as badges.

The Copperheads were critical of the wartime measures adopted by the Lincoln administration, such as conscription and the arrest and imprisonment of political opponents. They condemned Lincoln's Emancipation Proclamation, which came into force on January 1, 1863, not only because it made compromise with the Confederacy impossible, but because it represented an imposition of Northern—specifically Northeastern—values on the South.

Copperhead supporters

Copperhead feeling was strong in the border states of the Midwest, particularly where slavery continued. Midwestern farmers feared that the more industrial Northern states would come to dominate the Union, and that the agrarian economy and way of life of the Midwest would be lost.

The Copperheads saw the Lincoln administration as a puppet of New York capitalists and New England manufacturers. The Mississippi River blockade and the restriction of trade with the Confederacy plunged the Midwest into economic depression in 1861 and seemed to confirm such fears. Even Republicans recognized that Copperheadism in the Midwest was "not a question of loyalty, but … one of bread and butter."

The Copperheads' opposition to emancipation generated support among the working poor, especially recent immigrants. Among these groups racism was combined with fears that emancipation would result in a flood of cheap labor as former slaves came north. This would force down wages and possibly drive some out of work.

A political cartoon of 1860 depicting Peace Democrats as Copperhead snakes threatening the Union. Peace Democrats accepted their "Copperhead" nickname and took to wearing copper coins as badges.

PERSECUTION

Through 1863 rumors were rife that the Copperheads were planning insurrection and plotting in a secret society known as the Knights of the Golden Circle. Only a small fringe of Copperheads took part in secret activities. Republicans magnified this into a "Northwest Conspiracy" in which the Midwest planned to make a separate peace with the Confederacy. Republican propaganda succeeded in tarnishing the reputation of the Peace Democrats and provided the authorities with justification to suppress them. Copperheads were arrested, and some were sentenced to be hanged for treason. None were actually executed—they were jailed until the end of the war.

Clement L. Vallandigham, the leader of the Copperheads, was from Ohio and married to a Maryland planter's daughter. Many Copperheads came from border states, which shared economic and cultural ties with the Confederacy.

Opposing Republican war aims

While some Copperheads opposed the war entirely, and even plotted armed uprising, most were appalled at the idea of violent revolt. They concentrated on mobilizing anti-Lincoln opinion at the ballot box. A key Copperhead belief was that party politics and the democratic process should continue despite the war. Copperheads reminded voters that war should not be an excuse for dictatorship. They maintained political opposition to prevent such an outcome.

Clement L. Vallandigham

The most prominent Copperhead leader was Clement L. Vallandigham of Ohio. He blamed the Union for starting the war and was deported to the Confederacy in 1863 for asserting that the war was being fought to free blacks rather than to save the Union. He spent much of the rest of the war in exile in Canada. His arrest led to rioting in his hometown of Dayton, Ohio.

Falling support

Support for the Copperheads faded as the tide of the war turned in favor of the Union in the summer of 1863.

Although costly, the battles at Gettysburg and Vicksburg suggested that the North could win. Support for the Lincoln administration was buoyed by a wave of patriotism that swept through the Union. From his exile in Canada Vallandigham ran for the governorship of his home state of Ohio. The election was held in October 1863, and Vallandigham was defeated. After this failure many Copperheads realized, in the words of one supporter, "the people have voted in favor of the war and the way it is at present conducted."

Disheartened by resistance from the Union and Confederacy to compromise, cowed by arrests and treason trials, and at odds with the mood of the country, the Copperheads were largely silenced.

Costume and dress

The Civil War had a great effect on the way civilians dressed, particularly in the Confederacy. Southern women had to use all their ingenuity to make up for fabric shortages. They made dresses from drapes, spun cotton, and made dyes.

In the mid-19th century the clothes people wore clearly indicated their social class and wealth. While some fashions were common to all, the style of an outfit, the type of fabric, and how it was made differed greatly. Working men's and women's clothes were designed for practicality and durability. Wealthy people's wardrobes, by contrast, were designed around the social conventions of the day.

Women's clothes

All women had to wear many layers of clothing, including undergarments, a corset, a dress with fitted bodice, and a cape. Few would leave the house without a bonnet to cover their hair. Wealthy women had different outfits to suit the time of day and the social occasion. They had clothes for receiving guests at home, for visiting, for church, and for parties. Central to the fashionable costume of the day was a crinoline—a full skirt over a hooped wire frame (see box on page 64).

Hand sewn

Women of all classes in both the North and South were brought up to sew, knit, and embroider. Wealthy women spent part of each day working on some needle art or making the latest accessory. Magazines such as *Godey's Lady's Book* and *Peterson's Magazine* published the latest styles from Paris and London for their readers to either make or have made.

While rich families had most of their clothes made for them, less well-off women sewed and stitched clothes for themselves and their families. All clothes were hand sewn until the early 1850s, when Isaac Singer's sewing machine became widely available.

American women followed the latest fashions from Europe. This 1861 design by Jules David for an English magazine shows a white silk ball dress with hoop skirt and matching flowered coronet for the head.

The family of Ulysses S. Grant pictured after the war. The girl at the front wears a pinafore to keep her dress clean and a popular type of hat called a scholar, which has a ribbon hanging at the back.

HOMESPUN WOOL AND COTTON

"The Southern Girl with the Homespun Dress" was a popular wartime song with lyrics that extolled female sacrifice: "My homespun dress is plain; I know my hat's quite common too; But then it shows what Southern girls for Southern rights will do."

As new cloth became more scarce, women from every social class had to make their own fabric. This meant, for the most part, homespun wool and cotton. Patriotic rich Southerners dusted off their family spinning wheels and looms and undertook the dreary task of carding and spinning wool and cotton. Poor Southerners, who had always spun their own cloth, suddenly found their skills in great demand.

Homespun, although coarse, was acceptable when used for dresses, but as undergarments and nightgowns it was very uncomfortable. One Georgia lady, Eliza Andrews, wrote in her diary, "I can stand patched-up dresses, and even take a pride in wearing Confederate homespun, where it is done open and above board, but I can't help feeling vulgar and common in coarse underclothes."

Children's clothes

Both boys and girls were dressed in petticoats up until the age of five. After five, boys wore either short or long trousers or knickerbockers (baggy trousers gathered below the knee). Girls' dresses were made from cotton, calico, muslin, and in wealthier families, silk and linen. Children's clothes were designed to last, with seams that could be let out as the child grew. Clothes were not washed often, so girls covered their dresses with aprons or pinafores to keep them clean. Zippers had not been invented, so all clothing was fastened by buttons.

Men's clothes

Fashions in men's clothes did not change as quickly as those for women, and during the Civil War men made their civilian clothing last. Jackets and trousers were made of hard-wearing fabrics such as wool and were usually a plain dark color and occasionally plaid. Wealthy merchants and planters wore jackets of silk and linen.

In the North, New York and Boston were home to a growing garment industry, which produced ready-to-wear suits made by machine. Traditionally tailors cut, prepared, and finished a garment by hand. While wealthy Northern gentlemen and Southern planters continued to have their clothes custom-made by tailors, the less well-off took to the new, cheaper, mass-produced garments.

Men of all social classes always wore a vest and jacket. They were never seen in public in just a shirt. During the Civil War the sack coat became popular. It was more shapeless and looser than the more formal shawl-collared jacket. The sack coat was worn by both working men and those from the merchant classes. The quality of cloth was the difference.

Wartime shortages

Before the war the South relied on the North for manufactured cloth. The war closed off this trade, and cloth prices rose in the Confederacy. New fabric became hard to acquire, and Southern women resorted to homespinning, dyeing, and recycling household fabric. Homespun fabric, only worn by black slaves and poor whites before the war, became standard wear for all Southerners (see box opposite).

Northern women had to make economies in their dress as the war dragged on, but they were much less severe than in the South. For a small minority of Northern women, the wives and daughters of newly rich war contract merchants, money was plentiful, and they dressed in the latest fashions and fabrics. Southern women, who had been known for their style before the war, learned about the latest fashions not from Europe but from the invading Union troops.

Rising prices

As the war went on, the price of cloth in the Confederacy became unaffordable. In the fall of 1863 a dress that two years earlier had a price tag of $9 cost $195. By the end of the war a bolt of cloth sold for $45 a yard compared to $7 in 1861, and a spool of cotton or a book of pins cost $5 each.

1865 designs for hats and accessories. A woman in the 1860s rarely went out bare-headed. Casquettes, like those at the top of this fashion plate, were small winter hats decorated with velvet, fur, and feathers.

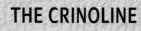
THE CRINOLINE

The crinoline, or hoop skirt, was a key fashion item for women in both the North and the South. The skirt first appeared in the 1840s. Its name came from the cotton or horsehair fabric used to make a stiff, full underskirt to hold out the skirt of the dress. In 1858 the fabric underskirt was replaced by a metal hoop frame tied at the waist.

The crinoline created a distinct shape that accentuated a woman's small waist, and it became popular with all social classes. Before the war the skirts had become increasingly full, sometimes as wide as 5 feet (1.5m) in diameter and requiring 20 yards (18m) of fabric. Only wealthy women could afford to follow the fashion to this extreme. For the working woman, who needed to move more freely, smaller hoops were more practical. In the 1860s the skirt gradually became flatter at the front and much smaller in diameter, with all the bulk at the back. It became more difficult to tell a woman's social class by the style of her dress.

One unexpected benefit of the hoop skirt during the war was its use as disguise. Some men dressed as women to evade enemy troops or to act as spies.

Mary Todd Lincoln, the wife of the president, pictured in 1861 wearing a fashionable full silk crinoline for a ball.

Southern ingenuity

In the novel *Gone with the Wind* by Margaret Mitchell Southern belle Scarlett O'Hara is so desperate for fabric that she creates a gown from living-room drapes. Women from the slaveholding classes made similar use of tablecloths and bedlinen, too. Southern women also made their own dyes. They made dark brown from walnut hulls, orange from sassafras roots, gray from the myrtle bush, green from the hickory tree, and red from cherry pits.

Toward the end of the war many Southerners were struggling to eat, let alone dress. They wore summer clothes well into the winter. Leather became scarcer and shoes impossible to find. Women sewed shoes out of cloth and paper, and their children went barefoot. Some women were housebound by their lack of footwear. Before the war slaves sometimes wore hand-me-downs from their mistresses. As the war went on, plantation women were sometimes forced to take back dresses they had given to their slaves.

The Civil War in the South changed women's clothing from being highly class segregated to more uniform. Women of all classes used initiative to clothe themselves and their families.

Cotton

In 1860 the South produced about 90 percent of the world's cotton. The Southern cotton crop accounted for half the exports of the United States by value, and newspapers and politicians in the South proclaimed that "Cotton is King."

The rise of cotton as the major crop of the South was rapid. Although the region had almost perfect climatic conditions for the cultivation of cotton, exports to Europe were modest until the beginning of the 19th century. The problem was that the cotton grown in the South was short staple, which meant that it had only short fibers. It was time-consuming and expensive to separate these short fibers from the cotton seeds in order to prepare the cotton for use in the textile industry.

The cotton gin

The problem was solved by the invention of the cotton gin in 1793. With a relatively simple contraption that was easy to manufacture and operate Eli Whitney mechanized the separation of the cotton fibers and the seeds. The cotton gin enabled the Southern planters to prepare the cotton crop for export quickly and efficiently. Where previously one person could clean the seeds from only about 1 pound (0.45kg) of cotton a day, "ginning" made it possible for an individual to clean up to 50 pounds (22.5kg) of cotton. In 1793, before the invention of the cotton gin, just 94 tons (85 tonnes) of cotton was harvested in the United States. By 1795 the cotton harvest was 3,000 tons (2,700 tonnes), and in 1810 it had reached 45,000 tons (40,800 tonnes).

Cotton and the conflict

American cotton was mainly produced by Southern planters who relied on slave labor, since free white labor was too expensive. The boom in cotton production brought a sharp rise in the number of slaves. In 1790 there were around 657,000 slaves in the Southern states. By 1860 there were 3.5 million slaves in the South. This expansion of the slave population did not find favor with abolitionists in the North.

Growing cotton depleted the soil, so new land for cotton production was

A cartoon showing John Bull (representing England) kneeling before King Cotton. Bull kneels on a slave, showing that those who bought Southern cotton turned a blind eye to the evil of slavery.

CONFEDERATE COTTON BONDS

In 1863 the Confederate government struck a deal with the French banking house of Emile Erlanger & Company. The bank agreed to sell $15 million worth of Confederate bonds (paper money) to private investors. The so-called Erlanger loan was unusual because the bonds were guaranteed not by gold but by "white gold"—cotton. Investors could exchange the bonds for cotton after the war at a good rate. The loan was hugely popular, attracting a host of high-profile investors in England, including the future prime minister, William Ewart Gladstone. The Confederate government used the money to buy vitally needed armaments and supplies for the troops.

North and South in the runup to the outbreak of hostilities. The cotton boom meant that the emancipation question was not just an issue of whether the existing Southern slave culture could be maintained, but whether it should be expanded both in terms of slave numbers and in territory. The extent to which cotton was behind the South's secession was illustrated by Alabama's state flag (adopted in January 1861), which pictured a cotton plant with a rattlesnake around it. The motto read *Noli Me Tangere*, meaning "Touch Me Not."

sought in the West. As cotton production spread, it exported a slave economy into regions that had not previously been cultivated or had been worked by free labor. It was this expansion of slavery into new areas that created dangerous tension between

Cotton as a weapon

Confederate politicians saw the cotton crop as a key weapon in their struggle against the Union. By withholding cotton from the textile manufacturers of the North, the South could damage the Union economy. By July 1862 only

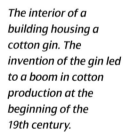

The interior of a building housing a cotton gin. The invention of the gin led to a boom in cotton production at the beginning of the 19th century.

around a quarter of the North's spindles were still in operation, and those manufacturers who were able to maintain production faced mounting costs as the price of raw cotton spiraled. Efforts were made to grow cotton within the Union, and cotton cultivation in Illinois met with moderate success. However, the quantities produced were negligible and Northern textile mills were largely brought to a standstill.

Despite the high prices that cotton could command in the North, Confederate patriots were eager to prevent Southern cotton from reaching the Union. Although there was undoubtedly some black-market trading of Confederate cotton in the North, some 2.5 million bales of cotton were burned either by their owners or by the Confederate armies in order to prevent them from falling into Northern hands as Union troops advanced.

Cotton diplomacy

Cotton was also seen by the South as a vital tool in its battle to gain international recognition of the Confederacy. President Jefferson Davis hoped that Britain and France might even be prepared to risk war with the Union in order to secure an uninterrupted supply of cotton. From 1861 the Southern planters initiated a voluntary but widespread embargo against cotton shipments to Europe.

More corn, less cotton

Deprived of their markets, many Southern planters moved from cultivating cotton to planting corn—it became a patriotic duty to grow food to feed the fledgling nation rather than cash crops. The cotton crop of 1861

had already been planted when hostilities broke out, and it yielded 4.5 million bales of cotton. In 1863 the American South produced fewer than half a million bales of cotton.

Misguided policy

Southern diplomatic logic was flawed. There had been bumper cotton crops in 1859 and 1860. By 1861 European mills were overstocked with raw cotton and unsold finished products, so the export embargo initially had little effect. It was not until 1863 that the "cotton famine" forced England's Lancashire mill workers onto short time. By then the Union blockade of the Southern coast was so effective that exports were difficult, even though a cash-strapped Confederacy was anxious to exchange cotton for military supplies in Europe. In fact, it was the export of cotton through the cotton bonds scheme (see box) that allowed the Confederacy to finance much of its military effort in the later years of the war.

Cotton bales are stored inside a Confederate fortification at Yorktown, Virginia. During the war the Confederates tried to prevent any Southern cotton from reaching the Union.

See also

- Abolition
- Agriculture
- Blockades and blockade-runners
- Causes of the conflict
- Economy of the South
- Foreign relations, Confederate
- Great Britain
- Slavery

Cumming, Kate

Kate Cumming (1835–1909) cared for Confederate soldiers from after the Battle of Shiloh in April 1862 until the end of the war. Her diary, a moving account of Confederate hospital life, was published in 1866.

Kate Cumming was born in Edinburgh, Scotland, in 1835 but emigrated with her family to North America. She was raised in Mobile, Alabama, where her father was a wealthy merchant. Cumming and her family were active members of St. John's Episcopal Church in Mobile.

Duty calls

In spring 1862 Kate Cumming volunteered as a nurse despite objections from her family that it was an unladylike undertaking. Until then she had never been inside a hospital, but she believed passionately that women from her social class should contribute to the Confederate war effort.

After the Battle of Shiloh, Tennessee, on April 6–7, 1862, where casualties were heavy, Kate began work comforting the wounded. She was based at the Tishomongo Hotel, where conditions were filthy, and most volunteers quit. Cumming recorded in her journal that she was too busy too change her bloodstained dress for 10 days. In the fall of 1863 she worked in Chattanooga, caring for those injured during the Chickamauga campaign. Her role was not so much nursing as managing the hospital and overseeing its laundry and kitchen.

Kate's diary

Kate Cumming's journal was a detailed account of life in Confederate hospitals. It was published in 1866 titled *A Journal of Hospital Life in the Confederate Army of Tennessee*. The work dealt with subjects such as the hostility nurses encountered from male physicians, food shortages, her own strong religious faith, and the plight of the wounded. Cumming's experience convinced her of war's brutality. She wrote, "These notes, often hurriedly penned amid the active duties of hospital life, but feebly indicate … the sad reality. I now pray … that men may beat their swords into plowshares and their spears into pruning hooks, and that nation may not lift a sword against nation, nor learn war anymore."

Later life

In 1874, after the war, Kate Cumming moved to Birmingham, Alabama, where she taught school. In 1890 she published *Gleanings from Southland*, a revised version of her journal. While the young Kate Cumming had blamed President Lincoln entirely for the war, this later work had a new, conciliatory tone toward the North. She died on June 5, 1909, in Birmingham.

Kate Cumming was a passionate supporter of the Confederate cause. When Virginia seceded, she wrote that she was "delirious with joy."

See also

- Chickamauga, Battle of
- Medicine
- Nurses and nursing
- Shiloh, Battle of
- Women and the war effort

Custer, George A.

General Custer (1839–1876) was a flamboyant Union cavalry officer who fought with distinction in the Civil War. He is best remembered, however, for leading his men to annihilation at the Battle of the Little Bighorn in 1876.

George Armstrong Custer was born in New Rumley, Ohio, in 1839 but moved as a child to Monroe, Michigan. In 1857 he enrolled in the U.S. Military Academy at West Point and graduated four years later—at the bottom of his class of 34. Despite his poor placing, Custer had graduated at the right time. He reported for duty and was sent with dispatches to General Irvin McDowell, who was in command of the Army of the Potomac. There he was assigned to duty as lieutenant in the 5th Cavalry. On the very day of his arrival he fought in the first major battle of the Civil War, at Bull Run on July 21, 1861.

Center of attention

From then on Custer was in the thick of the fighting, taking part in all but one of the battles fought by the Army of the Potomac. He gained a reputation for enthusiasm and bravery, and was promoted swiftly. By the war's end, aged only 25, Custer held a battlefield rank of major general. The "boy general," as he became known, also captured the public imagination with his striking image. He was dashingly good looking, with long golden hair set off by a bright red necktie and a custom-designed uniform dripping with gold braid. Neither his battlefield heroics nor his conspicuous appearance went uncriticized, however. Other generals

noted that units under Custer's command suffered high casualties. His vanity and arrogance annoyed many.

Custer's talent for always being at the center of the action continued to the end of the war. He pursued and harried the Confederate commander Robert E. Lee in the final days of the war and accepted the first flag of surrender in April 1865. He was also present at the surrender at Appomattox Court House.

After the war Custer sought further glory. In 1866 he was appointed lieutenant colonel of the newly formed 7th Cavalry in Kansas. He reveled in the 7th Cavalry's high-profile role, which was to batter the Plains Indians into submission and drive them onto reservations. Custer became a folk hero for his prowess as an Indian fighter. At the Battle of Little Bighorn on June 25, 1876, Custer and all 200 of his men died during an attack on a camp of Sioux and Cheyenne. The nation was stunned, and Custer was given a hero's burial at West Point. Later generations have been more critical of Custer.

See also

- Cavalry
- Military academies, North and South
- Potomac, Army of the
- Surrender of the Confederacy

General George Custer captured the first and the last battle flags of the Civil War.

Glossary

blockade-runner
A sailor or ship that broke through the Union blockade of Southern ports during the Civil War. Ships used in blockade-running were often specially built. They were fast and difficult to spot.

brevet rank
A promotion for an army officer to a higher rank, often as a honor just before retirement. There was no increase in pay and a limited increase in responsibilities.

brigade
A military unit consisting of between two and six regiments. The brigade was the common tactical unit of the Civil War.

casualty
A soldier lost in battle through death, wounds, sickness, capture, or missing in action. The huge number of casualties suffered by both sides during the Civil War—an estimated 620,000—was unprecedented.

commerce raider
A Confederate ship that targeted Union merchant shipping to undermine the North's ability to trade.

company
A military unit consisting of 50 to 100 men commanded by a captain. There were 10 companies in a regiment. Companies were raised by individual states.

conscription
Compulsory enrollment of able-bodied people into the armed forces, usually during a national emergency. Although unpopular, conscription was used by both the Union and the Confederacy.

corps
The largest military unit in the Civil War armies, consisting of two or more divisions. Corps were established in the Union army in March 1862 and in the Confederate army in November 1862.

division
The second largest military unit in the Civil War armies. A division was made up of three or four brigades and was commanded by a brigadier or major general. There were between two and four divisions in a corps.

habeas corpus
A legal protection against being imprisoned without trial. President Abraham Lincoln was severely criticized for suspending the right to trial in the Union during the war. President Jefferson Davis took a similar unpopular measure in the Confederacy.

mine
Known during the Civil War as "torpedoes," mines are explosive devices, usually concealed, designed to destroy enemy soldiers and transportation. Although considered at the time to be outside the bounds of acceptable warfare, they were used extensively in the Civil War.

mortar
A type of short-barreled cannon that threw shells in a high arc over enemy fortifications. They were usually used in siege warfare.

parole
Captured prisoners at the beginning of the war were exchanged and paroled, which meant they gave their word that they would not fight any more. The system became increasingly unworkable. Union authorities restricted the practice when they realized it was the main means by which the Confederacy replenished its troops.

partisan raiders
Irregular bands of troops, authorized by the Confederate government in April 1862 to operate behind enemy lines. They wore uniforms and were paid for captured war material they gave to the government. Despite some notable

successes, their overall usefulness to the Southern war effort has been disputed.

regiment
A military unit consisting of 10 companies of 100 men at full strength. In practice, however, most Civil War regiments were much smaller than this. Raised by state governors, they were usually composed of men from the same area. The Civil War soldier's main loyalty and sense of identity was connected to his regiment.

rifling
A technique used on both guns and cannons that allowed weapons to fire further and with greater accuracy than previously. Rifled barrels had spiral grooves cut into the inside, which gave a bullet or shell spin when fired.

secessionist
A person who supported the breaking away of the Southern states from the United States and thus a supporter of the Confederacy.

skirmishers
Infantrymen trained to fight in open order rather than the closed ranks of ordinary soldiers. They were often used ahead of the main force to prepare the way for a main attack or as snipers to harass an enemy counterattack.

sutler
A camp follower who sold provisions to the soldiers to supplement their army rations. Sutlers usually had a semi-official status and were attached to specific regiments. They were often resented for charging very high prices.

volunteer
A civilian who fights when his country goes to war, often because of personal convictions, a sense of adventure, or for a bounty or enlistment fee. The majority of Civil War soldiers were volunteers, rather than regular soldiers.

Further reading

Alleman, Tillie Pierce. *At Gettysburg, or What a Girl Saw and Heard of the Battle: A True Narrative.* New York: W. Lake Borland, 1889.

Berlin, Ira, et al. (editors). *Free at Last: A Documentary History of Slavery, Freedom, and the Civil War.* New York: The New Press, 1992.

Billings, John D. *Hardtack and Coffee, or the Unwritten Story of Army Life.* Boston: George M. Smith, 1887.

Bradford, Ned (editor). *Battles and Leaders of the Civil War.* New York: Dutton, 1956.

Catton, Bruce. *The Civil War.* Boston, MA: Houghton Mifflin, 1987.

Clark, Champ, and the editors of Time-Life Books. *The Assassination: Death of the President.* Alexandria, VA: Time-Life Books, 1987.

Coggins, Jack. *Arms and Equipment of the Civil War.* New York: Doubleday, 1962.

Damon, Duane. *When This Cruel War Is Over: The Civil War on the Home Front.* Minneapolis, MN: Lerner Publishing, 1996.

Engle, Stephen D. *The American Civil War: The War in the West 1861–July 1863.* London: Fitzroy Dearborn, 2001.

Evans, Charles M. *War of the Aeronauts.* Mechanicsburg, PA: Stackpole Books, 2002.

Faust, Patricia L. (editor). *Historical Times Illustrated Encyclopedia of the Civil War.* New York: Harper and Row, 1986.

Gallagher, Gary W. (editor). *The Wilderness Campaign.* Chapel Hill, NC: University of North Carolina Press, 1997.

Gallagher, Gary W. *The American Civil War: The War in the East 1861–May 1863.* London: Fitzroy Dearborn, 2001.

Gallagher, Gary W., and Robert Krick. *The American Civil War: The War in the East 1863–1865.* London: Fitzroy Dearborn, 2001.

Glatthaar, Joseph T. *The American Civil War: The War in the West 1863–1865.* London: Fitzroy Dearborn, 2001.

Grant, Ulysses S. *Personal Memoirs.* New York: Crescent Books, 1995.

Hendrickson, Robert. *The Road to Appomattox.* New York: John Wiley, 1998.

Kelbaugh, Ross J. *Introduction to Civil War Photography.* Gettysburg, PA: Thomas Publications, 1991.

McPherson, James M. *Battle Cry of Freedom.* New York: Oxford University Press, 1988.

Marrin, Albert. *Commander in Chief: Abraham Lincoln in the Civil War.* New York: Dutton, 1997.

Oates, Stephen B. *A Woman of Valor: Clara Barton and the Civil War.* New York: Macmillan/Free Press, 1994.

Robertson, James I. *Soldiers Blue and Gray.* Columbia, SC: University of South Carolina Press, 1998.

Schindler, Stanley (editor). *Memoirs of Robert E. Lee.* New York: Crescent Books, 1994.

Smith, Gene. *Lee and Grant: A Dual Biography.* New York: McGraw-Hill, 1984.

Trudeau, Noah. *Like Men of War: Black Troops in the Civil War, 1862–1865.* New York: Little, Brown, and Co, 1998.

Van Woodward, C. (editor). *Mary Chesnut's Civil War.* New Haven, CN: Yale University Press, 1981.

Wiley, Bell Irvin. *The Life of Johnny Reb: The Common Soldier of the Confederacy.* Baton Rouge, LA: Louisiana State University Press, 1980.

Wiley, Bell Irvin. *The Life of Billy Yank: The Common Soldier of the Union.* Baton Rouge, LA: Louisiana State University Press, 1981.

Wright, Mark. *What They Didn't Teach You about the Civil War.* Novato, CA: Presidio Press, 1996.

Useful websites:

These general sites have comprehensive links to a large number of Civil War topics:
http://sunsite.utk.edu/civil-war/warweb.html
http://civilwarhome.com/
http://americancivilwar.com/
http://www.civil-war.net/

http://www2.cr.nps.gov/abpp/battles/bystate.htm
This part of the National Parks Service site allows you to search for battles by state

http://pdmusic.org/civilwar.html
Sound files and words to Civil War songs

http://www.civilwarmed.org/
National Museum of Civil War Medicine

http://memory.loc.gov/ammem/aaohtml/exhibit/aopart4.html
Civil War section of the African American Odyssey online exhibition at the Library of Congress

http://valley.vcdh.virginia.edu/
The Valley of the Shadow Project: details of Civil War life in two communities, one Northern and one Southern

http://etext.lib.virginia.edu/civilwar/CivilWarBooks.html
Texts from the Civil War period online, including letters, poetry, and speeches

http://www.civilwarhome.com/records.htm
Battle reports by commanding generals from the Official Records

http://www.cwc.lsu.edu/
The United States Civil War Center at Lousiana State University

http://www.nps.gov/gett/getteducation/bcast20/act05.htm
Civil War slang

http://home.ozconnect.net/tfoen/
Original articles and images of the Civil War navies

http://civilwarmini.com/
Quizzes and interesting facts about the Civil War

Set Index

Page numbers in **bold** refer to volume numbers. Those in *italics* refer to picture captions, or where pictures and text occur on the same page.